This journal belongs to

_____

If found, please do the right thing!

The
DAILY
STOIC
JOURNAL

366 Days of Writing and Reflection on the Art of Living

RYAN HOLIDAY
AND STEPHEN HANSELMAN

PORTFOLIO
PENGUIN

INTRODUCTION

I n his tent at the front near the Granua River in the distant territory of Germania, the Emperor Marcus Aurelius rose at dawn. It was a struggle for him to get up this early, but he did anyway; his job required it. In the lamplight, he sat at the table and began to write in Greek in his journal about what the day ahead held in store for him. "I will encounter busybodies, ingrates, egomaniacs, liars, the jealous and cranks," he wrote to himself, preparing mentally for the inevitable difficulties of the life of an emperor, particularly one faced with leading an army and overseeing the empire from abroad.

But don't assume this was a complaint. There was not a note of frustration or resentment in his tone.

Marcus Aurelius was practicing with pleasure the philosophy he'd come to love and depend on, Stoicism. He was not writing off his fellow men and his subjects. On the contrary, in the completion of that thought, he would say of those busybodies and ingrates "that none can do me harm, or implicate me in ugliness—nor can I be angry at my relatives or hate them. For we are made for cooperation." And so he went about the rest of his morning journaling, writing little notes for himself on how to think, how to live, what to be grateful for, and then he proceeded on to meet the day, not simply as a philosopher, but as a true *philosopher king*.

If we can go back in time a little further, almost exactly one century and one evening before Marcus's morning meditation, we'd find another Stoic philosopher doing something quite similar. His name was Seneca, and he was alternatively a powerbroker, a playwright, and public intellectual serving at the highest levels in the court of Nero. Instead of journaling in the morning, he preferred to do his at night, putting, as he said, each day up for review. Seneca would look back on the day just then coming to a close and ask himself whether his actions had been just, what he could have done better, what habits he could curb, how he might improve himself. "We reflect upon that which we are about to do," he would tell his older brother about this nightly routine, "and yet our plans for the future descend from the past."

Reviewing the previous day is what helped Seneca prepare for the one that he would face the following morning.

Epictetus, another famous Stoic, was a former slave who lived a life not nearly as cushy or powerful as Seneca or Marcus, and would repeatedly remind his students to rehearse their lessons, to write them down for their own use. In *Discourses*, he says, "Every day and night keep thoughts like these at hand—write them, read them aloud, talk to yourself and others about them."

These then, the morning preparation and the evening review, are two of the most essential and intertwining exercises in Stoic philosophy and a tradition now more than two thousand years old. It's a tradition that you, in holding *The Daily Stoic Journal*, are now an heir to and can continue twice per day in your pursuit of the good life.

Unlike many other philosophies, Stoicism wasn't designed simply to be some explanation of the universe. It wasn't overly interested in complicated questions about where we came from or theoretical discussions of this issue or that one. Stoicism was designed by the Greeks and perfected by the Romans for the living and the *doing* of daily life for the man and woman trying to make it in a confusing world. As such, it was much more than a set of teachings or long-ago written sentences. It was instead a set of timeless practical exercises—systems for reducing fear, thoughts for battling destructive thoughts, reminders of things we take for granted, tools for resisting temptation, pillars of strength for tough moments. This meant that Stoicism wasn't something to be learned once or read once. It was meant to be studied and practiced.

Consider the title of Marcus Aurelius's only work, *Meditations*. He was *meditating*, to himself, for himself, on the philosophic principles he was still learning and practicing even in old age. A peek at Seneca's letters finds the same thing—he is writing to someone else, yes, but clearly the intended audience is also himself. He is thinking out loud. Epictetus, too, survives in the form of notes written by his student Arrian, and they read as if his day was spent trying to answer the endless questions of his students: What do I do about this? How can I handle something like that? Any advice for when I _____?

In our book *The Daily Stoic*, we tried to bring a collection of this wisdom to busy readers in a digestible and accessible way. Instead of translating and republishing the Stoics in their original form (which has been done quite well, many times), we created the first ever single-volume collection of all the great Stoics, arranged to highlight a thought from one each day. The response to the book was humbling and surprising. The book spent three months on the national bestseller lists and debuted in the form of a keynote address at what was likely the largest single gathering of Stoics in two thousand years. Our accompanying daily e-mail at DailyStoic.com was inundated with sign-ups, meaning that each morning tens of thousands of aspiring Stoics were all reading the same thing at the same time. We also began to see photos online from readers who had filled up the pages of *The Daily Stoic* and Moleskine journals with thoughts inspired by each day's meditation.

In response, we set out to create this journal, a companion guide to *The Daily Stoic* and a resource to anyone trying to practice the philosophy. We're honored that you now hold it in your hands.

HOW TO USE THIS JOURNAL

This book presents fifty-two Stoic disciplines or practices, one for each week of the year. Each practice is presented with some direction about its significance and application, along with a few quotes from the great Stoics to help focus your attention on the practice for the week—the first quote about each weekly practice is taken directly from that same week in *The Daily Stoic*. Each day presents a question to help you focus your morning preparations or evening review (or both). The questions will work for you whether you are reading along with *The Daily Stoic*, using our daily e-mail readings, or any other source.

We have not written a set of commandments or a step-by-step system that must be adhered to unthinkingly (if you don't want to respond to the prompts, ignore them and write about whatever you feel would be most beneficial. We also have suggestions at the back for other sources to use). As Seneca said: "The ones who pioneered these paths aren't our masters, but our guides. Truth stands open to everyone; it hasn't been monopolized."

The reason these Stoic practices have been so enduring (and are enjoying a modern-day resurgence) is that they are relentlessly focused on the situations that we face on a daily basis, what Richard Sorabji calls "the ordinary ups and downs of life, on bereavement, loss of office, promotion, the rat race, money, invasions, the sacking of cities, exile, worries about health." As the American philosopher Brand Blanshard marveled at Marcus Aurelius's legacy:

"Few care now about the marches and countermarches of the Roman commanders. What the centuries have clung to is a notebook of thoughts by a man whose real life was largely unknown who put down in the midnight dimness not the events of the day or the plans of the morrow, but something of far more permanent interest, the ideals and aspirations that a rare spirit lived by."

The Roman Stoics focused not on words, but action. As Seneca memorably put it, "Philosophy teaches us how to act, not how to talk." This bias toward improving our actions on a daily basis was something Epictetus made central to his teaching, summarized in his warning "not to be satisfied with mere learning, but to add practice and then training."

This journal is a place to focus your attention (*prosochē*) and practice (*meletē*) as you try to remember and apply what you are learning on the path to progress (*prokopē*). When you pursue the Stoic disciplines presented in this journal, each morning you will ask, as the great modern Stoic Pierre Hadot put it, "What principles will guide and inspire my actions?" And each evening you will examine where you fell short of those principles, as well as where you have made progress. You can begin on any calendar date you choose and proceed until the book is complete.

Together, the fifty-two ideals and aspirations offer something for every situation. Whether it's dealing with bad habits like complaining (Week XXXI), procrastination (Week XXXV), or panic (Week XXXIX), or finding less destructive alternatives to anger (Week XXIX), fear of the future (Week XXXIV), or dealing with haters (Week XXXVIII), you will find practical tools to put to use. You will gain powerful perspective by learning the exercise of taking "the view from above" (Week XXII), or learning to see things as others do (Week XI), and by taking on a role model (Week XXIII). You'll train yourself in the Stoic basics like the dichotomy of control (Week I), focus on the present moment (Week V), or how to test your impressions (Week XV).

It's important to remember this isn't a contest to see if you can live like some perfect sage or escape the correction of someone farther along the path than you. Anyone who uses philosophy that way is decidedly un-Stoic! As Seneca reminded us, "Let philosophy scrape off your own faults, rather than be a way to rail against the faults of others." Think of this journal as a brush for your own soul, just like brushing your teeth each morning and each evening.

The final lesson at the end of this book is the most essential one of all of Stoic philosophy: learning how to turn words into works. We hope you will make it that far, and if you do, we encourage you to start the same journey once again the following year, for you will be, as Heraclitus said, no longer the same person nor will this be the same book.

WEEK 1

WHAT'S UP TO US, WHAT'S NOT UP TO US

E pictetus's handbook (the *Enchiridion*) begins with the most powerful exercise in all of Stoicism: the distinction between the things
that are "up to us" (in our control) and the things that are "not up to
us." It is this, the dichotomy of control, that is the first principle in the
entire philosophy. We don't control many of the things we pursue in
life—yet we become angry, sad, hurt, scared, or jealous when we don't
get them. In fact, those emotions—those reactions—are about the only
thing that we do control. If that is the only lesson you journal about or
remember for this year, consider it a year well and philosophically
lived.

> "The chief task in life is simply this: to identify and separate mat-
> ters so that I can say clearly to myself which are externals not
> under my control, and which have to do with the choices I actu-
> ally control. Where then do I look for good and evil? Not to
> uncontrollable externals, but within myself to the choices that are
> my own . . ."
>
> —EPICTETUS, *DISCOURSES*, 2.5.4–5

> "Some things are in our control, while others are not. We control
> our opinion, choice, desire, aversion, and, in a word, everything
> of our own doing. We don't control our body, property, reputa-
> tion, position, and, in a word, everything not of our own doing.
> Even more, the things in our control are by nature free, unhin-
> dered, and unobstructed, while those not in our control are weak,
> slavish, can be hindered, and are not our own."
>
> —EPICTETUS, *ENCHIRIDION*, 1.1–2

> "We control our reasoned choice and all acts that depend on that
> moral will. What's not under our control are the body and any of
> its parts, our possessions, parents, siblings, children, or country—
> anything with which we might associate."
>
> —EPICTETUS, *DISCOURSES*, 1.22.10

January 1st   What things are truly in my control?

MORNING REFLECTION

EVENING REFLECTION

January 2nd   What am I learning and studying for?

MORNING REFLECTION

EVENING REFLECTION

January 3rd   What can I say no to so I can say yes to what matters?

MORNING REFLECTION

EVENING REFLECTION

January 4th   Am I seeing clearly? Acting generously? Accepting what I can't change?

MORNING REFLECTION

EVENING REFLECTION

January 5th   What is my purpose in life?

MORNING REFLECTION

EVENING REFLECTION

January 6th   Who am I and what do I stand for?

MORNING REFLECTION

EVENING REFLECTION

January 7th   How can I keep my mind clear from pollution?

MORNING REFLECTION

EVENING REFLECTION

WEEK II
THE SPHERE OF CHOICE

If the first step is to discern what is or isn't in our control, the second is to focus our energy on the things we have a choice about. The Stoics viewed the soul as a sphere that, when well tuned, well directed, was an invincible fortress against any trial or circumstance. Protected by our reason, this sphere of choice (*prohairesis*) is like a sacred temple and is the only thing we truly possess in life. We are the product of our choices, so it is essential then that we choose well. This week, consider and reflect on the choices you have: about your emotions, your actions, your beliefs, and your priorities.

> "Keep this thought at the ready at daybreak, and through the day and night—there is only one path to happiness, and that is in giving up all outside of your sphere of choice, regarding nothing else as your possession, surrendering all else to God and Fortune."
>
> —EPICTETUS, *DISCOURSES*, 4.4.39

> "Who then is invincible? The one who cannot be upset by anything outside their reasoned choice."
>
> —EPICTETUS, *DISCOURSES*, 1.18.21

> "The soul is a sphere, true to itself. It neither projects itself toward any external thing nor does it collapse on itself, but instead radiates a light which it shows itself the truth of all things and the truth in itself."
>
> —MARCUS AURELIUS, *MEDITATIONS*, 11.12

January 8th   What am I addicted to?

MORNING REFLECTION

EVENING REFLECTION

January 9th   If I don't control what happens to me, what is left?

MORNING REFLECTION

EVENING REFLECTION

January 10th   Where can I find steadiness?

MORNING REFLECTION

EVENING REFLECTION

January 11th   What are sources of unsteadiness in my life?

MORNING REFLECTION

EVENING REFLECTION

January 12th   Where is the path to serenity?

MORNING REFLECTION

EVENING REFLECTION

January 13th   What can I put outside my circle of control?

MORNING REFLECTION

EVENING REFLECTION

January 14th   What jerks me around?

MORNING REFLECTION

EVENING REFLECTION

WEEK III
THE WAKE UP

Each day you write in this journal, you'll be following in the footsteps of Epictetus, Marcus Aurelius, and all the other great Stoics. The Stoics did not face each day on a whim, but instead with preparation and discipline. They spent real time thinking and anticipating what was to come over the course of a day, a week, a year. Each morning activity—journaling included—was designed to make them ready to face the day. And with your work in this book, so you will be, too.

"Ask yourself the following first thing in the morning:

- What am I lacking in attaining freedom from passion?
- What for tranquility?
- What am I? A mere body, estate-holder, or reputation? None of these things.
- What, then? A rational being.
- What then is demanded of me? Meditate on your actions.
- How did I steer away from serenity?
- What did I do that was unfriendly, unsocial, or uncaring?
- What did I fail to do in all these things?"

—Epictetus, *Discourses*, 4.6.34–35

"On those mornings you struggle with getting up, keep this thought in mind—I am awakening to the work of a human being. Why then am I annoyed that I am going to do what I'm made for, the very things for which I was put into this world? Or was I made for this, to snuggle under the covers and keep warm? It's so pleasurable. Were you then made for pleasure? In short, to be coddled or to exert yourself?"

—Marcus Aurelius, *Meditations*, 5.1

January 15th   Am I staying the course or being steered away?

MORNING REFLECTION

EVENING REFLECTION

January 16th   What assumptions have I left unquestioned?

MORNING REFLECTION

EVENING REFLECTION

January 17th   Am I doing work that matters?

MORNING REFLECTION

EVENING REFLECTION

January 18th   Can I find grace and harmony in places others overlook?

MORNING REFLECTION

_____

_____

_____

_____

_____

_____

_____

_____

EVENING REFLECTION

_____

_____

_____

_____

_____

_____

_____

January 19th   Good or bad, high or low, do I still have choices?

MORNING REFLECTION

_____

_____

_____

_____

_____

_____

_____

EVENING REFLECTION

January 20th How can I rekindle my principles and start living today?

MORNING REFLECTION

EVENING REFLECTION

January 21st   What am I getting out of my journaling ritual?

MORNING REFLECTION

EVENING REFLECTION

WEEK IV
A LITTLE BETTER EVERY DAY

The Stoics saw their lives as works in progress. They didn't believe they were born perfect but they believed that with work, and dedication, they could get a little better every day. There is real delight in this progress, as Epictetus quoted by way of Socrates. Marcus Aurelius avidly pursued his own education and improvement, eagerly looking for advice from books, mentors, and historical examples. Follow that example this week, and see how you get a little better as each day passes.

We must keep constant watch over ourselves and, as Seneca phrased it, put each day up for review. Looking back on our day helps us to better understand where we may have fallen short and gives us tangible feedback for how to improve and grow. Only what you measure and record can be monitored; only what you put up for reflection can be learned from.

"I will keep constant watch over myself and—most usefully—will put each day up for review. For this is what makes us evil—that none of us looks back upon our own lives. We reflect upon only that which we are about to do. And yet our plans for the future descend from the past."

—SENECA, *MORAL LETTERS*, 83.2

"From Rusticus . . . I learned to read carefully and not be satisfied with a rough understanding of the whole, and not to agree too quickly with those who have a lot to say about something."

—MARCUS AURELIUS, *MEDITATIONS*, 1.7.3

"But what does Socrates say? 'Just as one person delights in improving his farm, and another his horse, so I delight in attending to my own improvement day by day.'"

—EPICTETUS, *DISCOURSES*, 3.5.14

January 22nd What bad habit did I curb today?

MORNING REFLECTION

EVENING REFLECTION

January 23rd Which of my possessions own me?

MORNING REFLECTION

EVENING REFLECTION

January 24th   Am I doing deep work?

MORNING REFLECTION

EVENING REFLECTION

January 25th   What do I truly prize?

MORNING REFLECTION

EVENING REFLECTION

January 26th   What is my mantra today?

MORNING REFLECTION

EVENING REFLECTION

January 27th   What am I studying, practicing, and training?

MORNING REFLECTION

EVENING REFLECTION

January 28th   What ruler do I measure myself against?

MORNING REFLECTION

EVENING REFLECTION

WEEK V
FOCUS ON THE PRESENT MOMENT

Marcus Aurelius ruled at a particularly turbulent time. Wars erupted on multiple fronts. Terrible plagues ravaged Rome. His rule was certainly one of constant, unrelenting pressure. But he never let it overwhelm him. From the Stoics and from the example of his adoptive father, the Emperor Antoninus Pius, Marcus found a coping strategy in always sticking close to the present moment and the duties at hand. When our own stress boils over, we can remember his practices and exercises, to stick with what is in front of us and not everything it might mean.

"At every moment keep a sturdy mind on the task at hand, as a Roman and human being, doing it with strict and simple dignity, affection, freedom, and justice—giving yourself a break from all other considerations. You can do this if you approach each task as if it is your last, giving up every distraction, emotional subversion of reason, and all drama, vanity, and complaint over your fair share. You can see how mastery over a few things makes it possible to live an abundant and devout life."

—MARCUS AURELIUS, *MEDITATIONS*, 2.5

"Were you to live three thousand years, or even a countless multiple of that, keep in mind that no one ever loses a life other than the one they are living, and no one ever lives a life other than the one they are losing. The longest and the shortest life, then, amount to the same, for the present moment lasts the same for all and is all anyone possesses. No one can lose either the past or the future, for how can someone be deprived of what's not theirs?"

—MARCUS AURELIUS, *MEDITATIONS*, 2.14

"Don't let your reflection on the whole sweep of life crush you. Don't fill your mind with all the bad things that might still happen. Stay focused on the present situation and ask yourself why it's so unbearable and can't be survived."

—MARCUS AURELIUS, *MEDITATIONS*, 8.36

January 29th   Am I keeping a sturdy mind on the task at hand?

MORNING REFLECTION

EVENING REFLECTION

January 30th   Am I content to be clueless about things that don't matter?

MORNING REFLECTION

EVENING REFLECTION

January 31st   What healing can philosophy help me find today?

MORNING REFLECTION

EVENING REFLECTION

February 1st   How can I conquer my temper?

MORNING REFLECTION

EVENING REFLECTION

February 2nd   What impulses rob me of self-control?

MORNING REFLECTION

EVENING REFLECTION

February 3rd   Am I in control or is my anxiety?

MORNING REFLECTION

EVENING REFLECTION

February 4th   Am I cultivating the invincibility of my power to choose?

MORNING REFLECTION

EVENING REFLECTION

WEEK VI
SUSPEND YOUR OPINIONS

E pictetus would teach that opinions were "the cause of a troubled mind." Opinions about the way we think things should be, need to be. One of the Stoic words for "opinion" is "dogma." The practice of Stoicism begins with a relentless attempt to suspend this dogmatic way of living—a cessation of the belief that you can force your opinions and expectations onto the world.

"We have the power to hold no opinion about a thing and to not let it upset our state of mind—for things have no natural power to shape our judgments."

—MARCUS AURELIUS, *MEDITATIONS*, 6.52

"Today I escaped from the crush of circumstances, or better put, I threw them out, for the crush wasn't from outside me but in my own assumptions."

—MARCUS AURELIUS, *MEDITATIONS*, 9.13

"There are two things that must be rooted out in human beings—arrogant opinion and mistrust. Arrogant opinion expects that there is nothing further needed, and mistrust assumes that under the torrent of circumstance there can be no happiness."

—EPICTETUS, *DISCOURSES*, 3.14.8

"Throw out your conceited opinions, for it is impossible for a person to begin to learn what he thinks he already knows."

—EPICTETUS, *DISCOURSES*, 2.17.1

February 5th   Am I thinking before I act?

MORNING REFLECTION

EVENING REFLECTION

February 6th   What needless conflict can I avoid?

MORNING REFLECTION

EVENING REFLECTION

February 7th How can I conquer fear and worry—before they conquer me?

MORNING REFLECTION

EVENING REFLECTION

February 8th   Do my outbursts ever make things better?

MORNING REFLECTION

EVENING REFLECTION

February 9th   What if I didn't have an opinion about this?

MORNING REFLECTION

EVENING REFLECTION

February 10th　What parts of my life are driven by anger?

MORNING REFLECTION

EVENING REFLECTION

February 11th   Is my soul a good ruler or a tyrant?

MORNING REFLECTION

EVENING REFLECTION

WEEK VII
WATCH OVER YOUR PERCEPTIONS

Every moment brings a flood of impressions of the world around us, and our minds are filled with the perceptions that arise with them. The Stoics teach us that we must keep a constant watch on this flood, as if we are standing guard to protect something of vital importance. What is it that we are protecting? Our peace of mind, clarity, and freedom—all of which are anchored in our perceptions. Epictetus reminds us that we need to pay attention to what matters and to learn how to ignore so many of the relentless provocations that come our way.

"Keep constant guard over your perceptions, for it is no small thing you are protecting, but your respect, trustworthiness and steadiness, peace of mind, freedom from pain and fear, in a word your freedom. For what would you sell these things?"

—EPICTETUS, *DISCOURSES*, 4.3.6b–8

"An important place to begin in philosophy is this: a clear perception of one's own ruling principle."

—EPICTETUS, *DISCOURSES*, 1.26.15

"I don't agree with those who plunge headlong into the middle of the flood and who, accepting a turbulent life, struggle daily in great spirit with difficult circumstances. The wise person will endure that, but won't choose it—choosing to be at peace, rather than at war."

—SENECA, *MORAL LETTERS*, 28.7

February 12th   For what have I sold my peace of mind?

MORNING REFLECTION

EVENING REFLECTION

February 13th   Which of my pleasures are really punishments?

MORNING REFLECTION

EVENING REFLECTION

February 14th   How can I do a better job listening to the little voice inside me?

MORNING REFLECTION

EVENING REFLECTION

February 15th   Do these strong emotions even make sense?

MORNING REFLECTION

EVENING REFLECTION

February 16th   What am I making harder than it needs to be?

MORNING REFLECTION

EVENING REFLECTION

February 17th   What happiness am I putting off that I could have right now?

MORNING REFLECTION

EVENING REFLECTION

February 18th   Am I in rigorous training against false impressions?

MORNING REFLECTION

EVENING REFLECTION

WEEK VIII
REDUCE WANTS, INCREASE HAPPINESS

The Stoics knew that wanting less increases gratitude, just as wanting more obliterates it. Epictetus focused much of his teaching on helping his students reduce the destructive habit of wanting more. In it he saw the key to a happy life and relationships. By practicing the art of wanting less and being grateful for the portion that we already have before us, we are hopping off the so-called hedonic treadmill and taking a real step on the path to a life of real contentment.

"Remember to conduct yourself in life as if at a banquet. As something being passed around comes to you, reach out your hand and take a moderate helping. Does it pass you by? Don't stop it. It hasn't yet come? Don't burn in desire for it, but wait until it arrives in front of you. Act this way with children, a spouse, toward position, with wealth—one day it will make you worthy of a banquet with the gods."

—EPICTETUS, *ENCHIRIDION*, 15

"When children stick their hand down a narrow goody jar they can't get their full fist out and start crying. Drop a few treats and you will get it out! Curb your desire—don't set your heart on so many things and you will get what you need."

—EPICTETUS, *DISCOURSES*, 3.9.22

"Freedom isn't secured by filling up on your heart's desire but by removing your desire."

—EPICTETUS, *DISCOURSES*, 4.1.175

February 19th   Am I happy with my portion at the banquet of life?

MORNING REFLECTION

EVENING REFLECTION

February 20th   Are the pleasures I'm chasing actually worth it?

MORNING REFLECTION

EVENING REFLECTION

February 21st   What can I stop yearning for?

MORNING REFLECTION

EVENING REFLECTION

February 22nd   Am I certain what I want to say isn't better left unsaid?

MORNING REFLECTION

EVENING REFLECTION

February 23rd   Why get angry at things, if anger doesn't change it?

MORNING REFLECTION

EVENING REFLECTION

February 24th　Why am I telling myself that I've been harmed?

MORNING REFLECTION

EVENING REFLECTION

February 25th   Will I even remember this fight in a few months?

MORNING REFLECTION

EVENING REFLECTION

WEEK IX
CULTIVATE INDIFFERENCE

Some people spend their lives chasing good things: health, wealth, pleasure, achievement. Others try to avoid the bad things with equal energy: sickness, poverty, pain. These look like two drastically different approaches but in the end, they are the same. The Stoics continually reminded themselves that so many of the things we desire and avoid are beyond our control. Instead of chasing impossibilities, the Stoics trained to be equally prepared and equally suited to thrive in either condition. They trained to be indifferent. This is a great power and the cultivation of this skill is a very powerful exercise.

"Of all the things that are, some are good, others bad, and yet others indifferent. The good are virtues and all that share in them; the bad are the vices and all that indulge them; the indifferent lie in between virtue and vice and include wealth, health, life, death, pleasure, and pain."

—EPICTETUS, *DISCOURSES*, 2.19.12b–13

"My reasoned choice is as indifferent to the reasoned choice of my neighbor, as to his breath and body. However much we've been made for cooperation, the ruling reason in each of us is master of its own affairs. If this weren't the case, the evil in someone else could become my harm, and God didn't mean for someone else to control my misfortune."

—MARCUS AURELIUS, *MEDITATIONS*, 8.56

"There are things in life which are advantageous and disadvantageous—both beyond our control."

—SENECA, *MORAL LETTERS*, 92.16

February 26th   Why do I need to care that someone else screwed up?

MORNING REFLECTION

EVENING REFLECTION

February 27th   How can I cultivate indifference to unimportant things?

MORNING REFLECTION

EVENING REFLECTION

February 28th   What would happen if I took a second to cool down?

MORNING REFLECTION

EVENING REFLECTION

February 29th
A Leap Year Day Mantra: You Can't Always Be Getting What You Want

March 1st   How often do I question the things others take for granted?

MORNING REFLECTION

EVENING REFLECTION

March 2nd   Do I see and assess myself accurately?

MORNING REFLECTION

EVENING REFLECTION

March 3rd   Am I standing with the philosopher or the mob?

MORNING REFLECTION

EVENING REFLECTION

March 4th How many of my limitations are really self-imposed?

MORNING REFLECTION

EVENING REFLECTION

WEEK X
WHAT EXPENSIVE THINGS COST

From the Cynics, the Stoics learned the powerful practice of focusing on the true worth (*axia*) of things. That the cost of an item isn't simply what it's sold for, but what it costs the owner to own. So much of our desire for material goods comes at the great price of both anxiety and the loss of our serenity—and even when gained, these things often leave us more anxious and less serene. This week, spend some time reflecting on what the things you buy actually cost. See if they are really worth what you have been paying.

"So, concerning the things we pursue, and for which we vigorously exert ourselves, we owe this consideration—either there is nothing useful in them, or most aren't useful. Some of them are superfluous, while others aren't worth that much. But we don't discern this and see them as free, when they cost us dearly."

—SENECA, *MORAL LETTERS*, 42.6

"If a person gave away your body to some passerby, you'd be furious. Yet you hand over your mind to anyone who comes along, so they may abuse you, leaving it disturbed and troubled—have you no shame in that?"

—EPICTETUS, *ENCHIRIDION*, 28

"Diogenes of Sinope said we sell things of great value for things of very little, and vice versa."

—DIOGENES LAERTIUS,
LIVES OF THE EMINENT PHILOSOPHERS, 6.2.35B

March 5th   Do I really need these things I work so hard for?

MORNING REFLECTION

EVENING REFLECTION

March 6th   Where am I a loud mouth?

MORNING REFLECTION

EVENING REFLECTION

March 7th   Can I test my own opinion before trusting it?

MORNING REFLECTION

EVENING REFLECTION

March 8th   Am I protecting my time and attention?

MORNING REFLECTION

EVENING REFLECTION

March 9th   Does my social circle make me better or worse?

MORNING REFLECTION

EVENING REFLECTION

March 10th   Who is my role model? Why?

MORNING REFLECTION

EVENING REFLECTION

March 11th   Where have I traded away freedom? How can I get it back?

MORNING REFLECTION

EVENING REFLECTION

WEEK XI
THINK ABOUT IT FROM THE OTHER
PERSON'S PERSPECTIVE

We tend to assume the best about our own intentions and the worst about other people's. Then we wonder why life is so full of conflict! The Stoics flipped this habit around, reminding themselves to be suspicious about their own first reaction and to approach others first with sympathy. Powerful people are often surprisingly terrible at behaving this way, but Marcus Aurelius, the most powerful man on earth during his reign, was renowned for his humanity in dealing with others. He told himself to always take a moment to remember his own failings and to contemplate how another might see a situation. He reminded himself, as we should, that most people are trying their best, even though that's easy to lose sight of in the rough and tumble of daily life. Let's remember that this week and think about each interaction from more than just our own point of view.

"Whenever someone has done wrong by you, immediately consider what notion of good or evil they had in doing it. For when you see that, you'll feel compassion, instead of astonishment or rage. For you may yourself have the same notions of good and evil, or similar ones, in which case you'll make an allowance for what they've done. But if you no longer hold the same notions, you'll be more readily gracious for their error."

—MARCUS AURELIUS, *MEDITATIONS*, 7.26

"When your sparring partner scratches or head-butts you, you don't then make a show of it, or protest, or view him with suspicion or as plotting against you. And yet you keep an eye on him, not as an enemy or with suspicion, but with a healthy avoidance. You should act this way with all things in life. We should give a pass to many things with our fellow trainees. For, as I've said, it's possible to avoid without suspicion or hate."

—MARCUS AURELIUS, *MEDITATIONS*, 6.20

March 12th   What would change if I looked for other people's good intentions?

MORNING REFLECTION

EVENING REFLECTION

March 13th   Instead of calling it bad luck, can I come to see it as inevitable?

MORNING REFLECTION

EVENING REFLECTION

March 14th   How is my arrogance preventing me from learning?

MORNING REFLECTION

EVENING REFLECTION

March 15th   What would it be like if I focused entirely on the present moment?

MORNING REFLECTION

EVENING REFLECTION

March 16th   Do I appreciate this mind I have been given?

MORNING REFLECTION

EVENING REFLECTION

March 17th   Are my choices beautiful?

MORNING REFLECTION

EVENING REFLECTION

March 18th   What bad assumptions can I cast out?

MORNING REFLECTION

EVENING REFLECTION

WEEK XII
THE PORTABLE RETREAT

It is in the future—on a vacation, on our day off, when we plan to get out into nature—that we think we'll find peace and release from the crush of the everyday demands of life. Yet this never seems to really happen as often as we think, does it? And when we do get that peace, it is difficult to keep once we're back in the fray. For a Stoic, all of this is madness. The true retreat is to the freedom of our own mind and soul, to consider the gifts we already have that can be our refuge for all time. If we take the time, daily, to do so.

"People seek retreats for themselves in the country, by the sea, or in the mountains. You are very much in the habit of yearning for those same things. But this is entirely the trait of a base person, when you can, at any moment, find such a retreat in yourself. For nowhere can you find a more peaceful and less busy retreat than in your own soul—especially if on close inspection it is filled with ease, which I say is nothing more than being well-ordered. Treat yourself often to this retreat and be renewed."

—MARCUS AURELIUS, *MEDITATIONS*, 4.3.1

"Remember that it's not only the desire for wealth and position that debases and subjugates us, but also the desire for peace, leisure, travel, and learning. It doesn't matter what the external thing is, the value we place on it subjugates us to another . . . where our heart is set, there our impediment lies."

—EPICTETUS, *DISCOURSES*, 4.4.1–2; 15

"Remember that your ruling reason becomes unconquerable when it rallies and relies on itself, so that it won't do anything contrary to its own will, even if its position is irrational. How much more unconquerable if its judgments are careful and made rationally? Therefore, the mind freed from passions is an impenetrable fortress—a person has no more secure place of refuge for all time."

—MARCUS AURELIUS, *MEDITATIONS*, 8.48

March 19th   What is the real cause of my irritations—external things or my opinions?

MORNING REFLECTION

EVENING REFLECTION

March 20th   Am I cultivating the virtue that makes adversity bearable?

MORNING REFLECTION

EVENING REFLECTION

March 21st   What if I sought peace where I am right now instead of in distant lands?

MORNING REFLECTION

EVENING REFLECTION

March 22nd   Have I confused schooling and *education*?

MORNING REFLECTION

EVENING REFLECTION

March 23rd   How can I treat my greedy vices? How can I heal my sickness?

MORNING REFLECTION

EVENING REFLECTION

March 24th What philosophical lessons can I find in ordinary things?

MORNING REFLECTION

EVENING REFLECTION

March 25th   Would I feel wealthier if I decreased my wants?

MORNING REFLECTION

EVENING REFLECTION

WEEK XIII
SAY NO TO THE NEED TO IMPRESS

If the desire to impress and be liked by others is innate to humans as a species, then every generation born before social media got off lucky. Today we face an unending stream of status updates demanding to be filled with all the impressive things we are doing, the trials we are overcoming, announcements of our dangers averted and triumphs realized. It's exhausting. Centuries ago, Epictetus saw this pride and narcissism even in his (computerless) students and reminded them it wasn't so innocent. In fact, he told them that it would destroy their life's purpose, it would distract and fatigue them. Seneca, too, saw this seeking of the approval of spectators as one of life's disgraces. Watch those impulses this week, notice how much you seem to need your phone and status updates and then ask: Is this the kind of person I want to be? Is this what a philosopher would do?

"If you should ever turn your will to things outside your control in order to impress someone, be sure that you have wrecked your whole purpose in life. Be content, then, to be a philosopher in all that you do, and if you wish also to be seen as one, show yourself first that you are and you will succeed."
—EPICTETUS, *ENCHIRIDION*, 23

"In public avoid talking often and excessively about your accomplishments and dangers, for however much you enjoy recounting your dangers, it's not so pleasant for others to hear about your affairs."
—EPICTETUS, *ENCHIRIDION*, 33.14

"How disgraceful is the lawyer whose dying breath passes while at court, at an advanced age, pleading for unknown litigants and still seeking the approval of ignorant spectators."
—SENECA, *ON THE BREVITY OF LIFE*, 20.2

March 26th   Am I keeping watch?

MORNING REFLECTION

EVENING REFLECTION

March 27th   What valuable things do I sell too cheaply?

MORNING REFLECTION

EVENING REFLECTION

March 28th   Is my training designed to help me rise to the occasion?

MORNING REFLECTION

EVENING REFLECTION

March 29th   Why do I care so much about impressing people?

MORNING REFLECTION

EVENING REFLECTION

March 30th   If I'm not ruled by reason, what am I ruled by?

MORNING REFLECTION

EVENING REFLECTION

March 31st Can I stop chasing the impossible today?

MORNING REFLECTION

EVENING REFLECTION

April 1st   What thoughts are coloring my world?

MORNING REFLECTION

EVENING REFLECTION

WEEK XIV
WHAT CAN GO WRONG . . . MIGHT

We call the people who dwell on what might go wrong "pessimists." Some even think that bad thoughts attract bad events. The Stoics found this all to be nonsense. In fact, they had a practice of *praemeditatio malorum* (premeditation of evils) that specifically encouraged musing on the so-called worst-case scenario. Marcus would begin his day thinking about all the ugliness he would see on display at court—not for the purpose of working himself up, but precisely the opposite, to calm and focus himself to be prepared to act in the proper way rather than to react. Seneca, too, practiced meditating in advance, not only about what normally happens, but what could happen. Epictetus went as far as to imagine losing a loved one every time he would kiss them. The Stoics believed all that we have is on loan from Fortune, and that negative visualization helps increase our awareness of the unexpected—don't shy away from this in your thoughts.

> "When you first rise in the morning tell yourself: I will encounter busybodies, ingrates, egomaniacs, liars, the jealous and cranks. They are all stricken with these afflictions because they don't know the difference between good and evil. Because I have understood the beauty of good and the ugliness of evil, I know that these wrongdoers are still akin to me . . . and that none can do me harm, or implicate me in ugliness—nor can I be angry at my relatives or hate them. For we are made for cooperation."
>
> —MARCUS AURELIUS, *MEDITATIONS*, 2.1

> "Being unexpected adds to the weight of a disaster, and being a surprise has never failed to increase a person's pain. For that reason, nothing should ever be unexpected by us. Our minds should be sent out in advance to all things and we shouldn't just consider the normal course of things, but what could actually happen. For is there anything in life that Fortune won't knock off its high horse if it pleases her?"
>
> —SENECA, *MORAL LETTERS*, 91.3A–4

April 2nd   What can I do today to keep drama away?

MORNING REFLECTION

EVENING REFLECTION

April 3rd   Are my plans at war with my other plans?

MORNING REFLECTION

EVENING REFLECTION

April 4th   Can I fight to be the person philosophy wants me to be today?

MORNING REFLECTION

EVENING REFLECTION

April 5th   What would happen if I stopped to verify my opinions and initial reactions?

MORNING REFLECTION

EVENING REFLECTION

April 6th   Despite the worst things people do, can I love them anyway?

MORNING REFLECTION

EVENING REFLECTION

April 7th   Where are my opinions part of the problem?

MORNING REFLECTION

EVENING REFLECTION

April 8th   What bad assumptions, habits, or advice have I accepted?

MORNING REFLECTION

EVENING REFLECTION

WEEK XV
TEST YOUR IMPRESSIONS

One of Epictetus's key teachings was about testing all our impressions—any experience, perception, or circumstance that we find in front of us. He uses a key verb to emphasize this practice, *dokimázō*, ten times in the *Discourses* and once in the opening of the *Enchiridion*. The word carries the meaning of the assayer, one who tests fine metals and coins to verify their authenticity. In one of the most memorable uses Epictetus compares our need to test impressions to what is done with coins and how the skilled merchant can hear a counterfeit coin cast upon a table just as a musician would detect a sour note. This week, let us go through the exercise of assaying everything that comes before us, assuming it all to be counterfeit or misleading until we can prove otherwise.

"When it comes to money, where we feel our clear interest, we have an entire art where the tester uses many means to discover the worth . . . just as we give great attention to judging things that might steer us badly. But when it comes to our own ruling principle, we yawn and doze off, accepting any appearance that flashes by without counting the cost."

—EPICTETUS, *DISCOURSES*, 1.20.8; 11

"First off, don't let the force of the impression carry you away. Say to it, 'hold up a bit and let me see who you are and where you are from—let me put you to the test.' . . ."

—EPICTETUS, *DISCOURSES*, 2.18.24

"From the very beginning, make it your practice to say to every harsh impression, 'you are an impression and not at all what you appear to be.' Next, examine and test it by the rules you possess, the first and greatest of which is this—whether it belongs to the things in our control or not in our control, and if the latter, be prepared to respond, 'It is nothing to me.'"

—EPICTETUS, *ENCHIRIDION*, 1.5

April 9th   Can I step back and test my impressions? What would I find if I did?

MORNING REFLECTION

EVENING REFLECTION

April 10th   How do my judgments cause me anguish?

MORNING REFLECTION

EVENING REFLECTION

April 11th　Can I stop thinking I already know and learn something here?

MORNING REFLECTION

EVENING REFLECTION

April 12th   What's the truth about so-called "honors" and "riches"?

MORNING REFLECTION

EVENING REFLECTION

April 13th   What would *less* look like?

MORNING REFLECTION

EVENING REFLECTION

April 14th   Do I balance my life better than the balance sheet of my business?

MORNING REFLECTION

EVENING REFLECTION

April 15th   Life is full of taxes—am I prepared to pay them?

MORNING REFLECTION

EVENING REFLECTION

WEEK XVI
IMPULSE CONTROL

I f something is making you upset, write it here and look at it. What happened? Who caused it? Now think about your reaction: What did you say? What did you feel? Did this make it better or worse? Marcus Aurelius, as emperor, clearly had many people and causes to be upset about. He also had real power and authority. Even so we find that he would tell himself, "You have power over your mind—not outside events. Realize this, and you will find strength." So, too, with what has happened to you—you did not control what happened, but you do control which impulses you follow in the wake of it.

"Epictetus says we must discover the missing art of assent and pay special attention to the sphere of our impulses—that they are subject to reservation, to the common good, and that they are in proportion to actual worth."
—MARCUS AURELIUS, *MEDITATIONS*, 11.37

"You say, good fortune used to meet you at every corner. But the fortunate person is the one who gives themselves a good fortune. And good fortunes are a well-tuned soul, good impulses, and good actions."
—MARCUS AURELIUS, *MEDITATIONS*, 5.36

"Frame your thoughts like this—you are an old person, you won't let yourself be enslaved by this any longer, no longer pulled like a puppet by every impulse, and you'll stop complaining about your present fortune or dreading the future."
—MARCUS AURELIUS, *MEDITATIONS*, 2.2

April 16th   What can I pay closer attention to today?

MORNING REFLECTION

EVENING REFLECTION

April 17th   Can I stop feeling hurt by every little thing?

MORNING REFLECTION

EVENING REFLECTION

April 18th   Do I need to have an opinion about this?

MORNING REFLECTION

EVENING REFLECTION

April 19th   Am I leaving room for what might happen?

MORNING REFLECTION

EVENING REFLECTION

April 20th   What are the few real goods?

MORNING REFLECTION

EVENING REFLECTION

April 21st How long can I go without letting my attention slide?

MORNING REFLECTION

EVENING REFLECTION

April 22nd   Am I self-aware, self-critical, and self-determining?

MORNING REFLECTION

EVENING REFLECTION

WEEK XVII
THE FREEDOM OF CONTEMPT

The language we use to describe things imputes value to those things. We often embellish our language with superlatives to help make our choices of what to buy, wear, eat, or drink seem much better than they really are. As emperor, Marcus Aurelius could have the finest Falernian wine at his table at any meal—but he preferred to remind himself it was only grape juice. As emperor, he was the only Roman allowed to wear a purple cloak, but he took pains to point out that his cloak was like any other, just dyed with shellfish blood to produce the purple hue. This week, practice cutting your own luxuries and the things you yearn for down to size with a little contempt. Describe them with the bluntest language you can—and see how much their power over you diminishes.

> "Just as when meat or other foods are set before us we think, this is a dead fish, a dead bird or pig; and also, this fine wine is only the juice of a bunch of grapes, this purple-edged robe just sheep's wool dyed in a bit of blood from a shellfish; or of sex, that it is only rubbing private parts together followed by a spasmic discharge—in the same way our impressions grab actual events and permeate them, so we see them as they really are."
> —MARCUS AURELIUS, *MEDITATIONS*, 6.13

> "Keep a list before your mind of those who burned with anger and resentment about something, of even the most renowned for success, misfortune, evil deeds, or any special distinction. Then ask yourself, how did that work out? Smoke and dust, the stuff of simple myth trying to be legend . . ."
> —MARCUS AURELIUS, *MEDITATIONS*, 12.27

> "You know what wine and liqueur tastes like. It makes no difference whether a hundred or a thousand bottles pass through your bladder—you are nothing more than a filter."
> —SENECA, *MORAL LETTERS*, 77.16

April 23rd   How am I caring for my mind?

MORNING REFLECTION

EVENING REFLECTION

April 24th   Nice cars, jewels, fine wine—what are these things really?

MORNING REFLECTION

EVENING REFLECTION

April 25th　Am I willing to admit when I'm wrong?

MORNING REFLECTION

EVENING REFLECTION

April 26th   How can I learn from my sparring partners?

MORNING REFLECTION

EVENING REFLECTION

April 27th   How long does praise really last anyway?

MORNING REFLECTION

EVENING REFLECTION

April 28th   What power does all my wanting take from me?

MORNING REFLECTION

EVENING REFLECTION

April 29th   What do I feel when I look up at the sky?

MORNING REFLECTION

EVENING REFLECTION

WEEK XVIII
SHOW, DON'T TELL

The art of living isn't a set of teachings or a formula we can memorize. It's a practice that requires constant work. Epictetus was constantly reminding his students not to parrot back what they'd heard in the lecture hall or read in books, but to put it to work in practice. He knew that progress you could see was better than any proclaimed. Let your writing this week exhibit what you have done and what you are doing, not on what you plan to do or think you are. Let it be a catalog of your actions—good actions.

"Those who receive the bare theories immediately want to spew them, as an upset stomach does its food. First digest your theories and you won't throw them up. Otherwise they will be raw, spoiled, and not nourishing. After you've digested them, show us the changes in your reasoned choices, just like the shoulders of gymnasts display their diet and training, and as the craft of artisans show in what they've learned."

—Epictetus, *Discourses*, 3.21.1–3

"First practice not letting people know who you are—keep your philosophy to yourself for a bit. In just the manner that fruit is produced—the seed buried for a season, hidden, growing gradually so it may come to full maturity. But if the grain sprouts before the stalk is fully developed, it will never ripen. . . . That is the kind of plant you are, displaying fruit too soon, and the winter will kill you."

—Epictetus, *Discourses*, 4.8.35b–37

April 30th   Do my actions match my character?

MORNING REFLECTION

EVENING REFLECTION

May 1st   Do my actions—and my mind—match my philosophy?

MORNING REFLECTION

EVENING REFLECTION

May 2nd What kind of person do I want to be?

MORNING REFLECTION

EVENING REFLECTION

May 3rd   Am I showing or telling?

MORNING REFLECTION

EVENING REFLECTION

May 4th   Where can I spend money to help others?

MORNING REFLECTION

EVENING REFLECTION

May 5th   Have I made myself a lifelong project?

MORNING REFLECTION

EVENING REFLECTION

May 6th   Am I seeking the beauty of human excellence?

MORNING REFLECTION

EVENING REFLECTION

The Roman Stoics put a heavy emphasis on dealing with habitual behavior in order to make progress in the art of living. The great Roman Stoic educator Musonius Rufus held that all the theory in the world couldn't trump good habits (or overcome bad habits). Epictetus followed Musonius in this focus on habit, with an eye to not reinforcing bad habits—such as anger—and finding a way to replace them with better ones. We all recognize bad habits when we see them in others, but it's a little harder to see them in ourselves. This week meditate on the habits or recurring behaviors that are holding you back—even ask someone close to you to help.

"Every habit and capability is confirmed and grows in its corresponding actions, walking by walking, and running by running . . . therefore, if you want to do something, make a habit of it; if you don't want to do that, don't, but make a habit of something else instead. The same principle is at work in our state of mind. When you get angry, you've not only experienced that evil, but you've also reinforced a bad habit, adding fuel to the fire."

—EPICTETUS, *DISCOURSES*, 2.18.1–5

"If you don't wish to be a hothead, don't feed your habit. Try as a first step to remain calm and count the days you haven't been angry. I used to be angry every day, now every other day, then every third or fourth . . . if you make it as far as thirty days, thank God! For habit is first weakened and then obliterated. When you can say 'I didn't lose my temper today, or the next day, or for three or four months, but kept my cool under provocation,' you will know you are in better health."

—EPICTETUS, *DISCOURSES*, 2.18.11B–14

"What assistance can we find in the fight against habit? Try the opposite!"

—EPICTETUS, *DISCOURSES*, 1.27.4

May 7th   What is some good I can get from myself today?

MORNING REFLECTION

EVENING REFLECTION

May 8th   What evil comes from my own choices?

MORNING REFLECTION

EVENING REFLECTION

May 9th   Will I seize this day?

MORNING REFLECTION

EVENING REFLECTION

May 10th   What bold thing can I do today?

MORNING REFLECTION

EVENING REFLECTION

May 11th   Where does my lack of self-control create problems?

MORNING REFLECTION

EVENING REFLECTION

May 12th   What would happen if I responded with kindness, no matter what?

MORNING REFLECTION

EVENING REFLECTION

May 13th   Which bad habits am I fueling?

MORNING REFLECTION

EVENING REFLECTION

WEEK XX
COUNT YOUR BLESSINGS

I t's easy to complain about the things missing in our lives, and so much harder to appreciate how much we already have. Seneca reminded us that everything we need to be happy is right in front of us, while the luxuries we might be missing would themselves come at great cost—at the cost of what we already have. Marcus agreed, and reminded himself to count those blessings present in our lives and to imagine what it would be like to not have them (and how much we would miss them). List your blessings this week, take conscious note of what you are fortunate to have and enjoy, so you can see clearly, as Epictetus put it, where they came from and feel a sense of gratitude for that.

"Don't set your mind on things you don't possess as if they were yours, but count the blessings you actually possess and think how much you would desire them if they weren't already yours. But watch yourself, that you don't value these things to the point of being troubled if you should lose them."

—MARCUS AURELIUS, *MEDITATIONS*, 7.27

"The founder of the universe, who assigned to us the laws of life, provided that we should live well, but not in luxury. Everything needed for our well-being is right before us, whereas what luxury requires is gathered by many miseries and anxieties. Let us use this gift of nature and count it among the greatest things."

—SENECA, *MORAL LETTERS*, 119.15b

"It is easy to praise providence for anything that may happen if you have two qualities: a complete view of what has actually happened in each instance and a sense of gratitude. Without gratitude what is the point of seeing, and without seeing what is the object of gratitude?"

—EPICTETUS, *DISCOURSES*, 1.6.1–2

May 14th   Are my actions contributing to my well-being?

MORNING REFLECTION

EVENING REFLECTION

May 15th   What blessings can I count right now?

MORNING REFLECTION

EVENING REFLECTION

May 16th   How am I creating momentum for my good habits?

MORNING REFLECTION

EVENING REFLECTION

May 17th   Am I on the path to progress?

MORNING REFLECTION

EVENING REFLECTION

May 18th   Is my attention actually on the things at hand?

MORNING REFLECTION

EVENING REFLECTION

May 19th   Where am I doing the opposite of what I should?

MORNING REFLECTION

EVENING REFLECTION

May 20th   What are the seeds I'm planting and what will they grow?

MORNING REFLECTION

EVENING REFLECTION

WEEK XXI
PRACTICE TRUE JOY

The Stoics held joy (*chara*) to be one of the good passions, worthy of practice in everyday life. But Stoic joy isn't about the delights of the senses or material pleasure. To Marcus, joy was being kind to others. To Seneca, it was freedom from fear of suffering and death. Let's laugh with Democritus, as Seneca says, and engage in our "proper human work" with joy. Consider in your writing this week where you might find joy and what good you might do with it.

"Joy for human beings lies in proper human work. And proper human work consists in: acts of kindness to other human beings, disdain for the stirrings of the senses, identifying trustworthy impressions, and contemplating the natural order and all that happens in keeping with it."

—MARCUS AURELIUS, *MEDITATIONS*, 8.26

"Trust me, real joy is a serious thing. Do you think someone can, in the charming expression, blithely dismiss death with an easy disposition? Or swing open the door to poverty, keep pleasures in check, or meditate on the endurance of suffering? The one who is comfortable with turning these thoughts over is truly full of joy, but hardly cheerful. It's exactly such a joy that I would wish for you to possess, for it will never run dry once you've laid claim to its source."

—SENECA, *MORAL LETTERS*, 23.4

"Heraclitus would shed tears whenever he went out in public—Democritus laughed. One saw the whole as a parade of miseries, the other of follies. And so, we should take a lighter view of things and bear them with an easy spirit, for it is more human to laugh at life than to lament it."

—SENECA, *ON TRANQUILITY OF MIND*, 15.2

May 21st   Can I take a blow and stay in the ring?

MORNING REFLECTION

EVENING REFLECTION

May 22nd   Can I be a good person right here, right now?

MORNING REFLECTION

EVENING REFLECTION

May 23rd　Can I start living right here, right now?

MORNING REFLECTION

EVENING REFLECTION

May 24th   How can I make my own good fortune?

MORNING REFLECTION

EVENING REFLECTION

May 25th   What kind or selfless things will bring me joy?

MORNING REFLECTION

EVENING REFLECTION

May 26th   What if I stopped caring what others thought?

MORNING REFLECTION

EVENING REFLECTION

May 27th   What small stuff should I sweat?

MORNING REFLECTION

EVENING REFLECTION

WEEK XXII
THE VIEW FROM ABOVE

The way to escape petty concerns and worries of daily existence requires taking some time out and getting what Stoics like to call "the view from above." This was something Marcus Aurelius reminded himself to do regularly. He had learned from Heraclitus that everything in the world was constantly changing and that remembering this can eliminate so many stresses and concerns. This week don't just look at what you're dealing with in your life up close; try to see it from far away, too. Try to describe what another, larger perspective would look like—of your problems, of your worries, of your obsessions.

"How beautifully Plato put it. Whenever you want to talk about people, it's best to take a bird's-eye view and see everything all at once—of gatherings, armies, farms, weddings and divorces, births and deaths, noisy courtrooms or silent spaces, every foreign people, holidays, memorials, markets—all blended together and arranged in a pairing of opposites."

—MARCUS AURELIUS, *MEDITATIONS*, 7.48

"Watch the stars in their courses and imagine yourself running alongside them. Think constantly on the changes of the elements into each other, for such thoughts wash away the dust of earthly life."

—MARCUS AURELIUS, *MEDITATIONS*, 7.47

"The cosmic order—the same for everyone—wasn't made by any god or human, but always was and always will be. An eternal fire, kindled in measures, and extinguished in measures."

—HERACLITUS (AS QUOTED BY CLEMENT OF ALEXANDRIA)

May 28th   What should I think about before I take action?

MORNING REFLECTION

EVENING REFLECTION

May 29th   What work nourishes my mind?

MORNING REFLECTION

EVENING REFLECTION

May 30th   Is my hard work for the right end?

MORNING REFLECTION

EVENING REFLECTION

May 31st   If my vocation is to be a good person, am I doing a good job?

MORNING REFLECTION

EVENING REFLECTION

June 1st   Do I have a backup option in mind for all things?

MORNING REFLECTION

EVENING REFLECTION

June 2nd   Where have I lost the forest for the trees?

MORNING REFLECTION

EVENING REFLECTION

June 3rd   Do I have a backup plan for my backup plan?

MORNING REFLECTION

EVENING REFLECTION

WEEK XXIII
ROLE MODELS

Adoption was a widespread practice in Roman society, especially in the senatorial class and as a provision for imperial succession. Marcus Aurelius himself was the adopted son of Emperor Antoninus Pius, who himself was adopted by the Emperor Hadrian so that Marcus would one day succeed them both to the purple. While Seneca was never adopted, his brother Novatus was, becoming Gallio who in the New Testament refused to press charges on Saint Paul. But Seneca liked to look at the phenomenon of adoption the other way around, saying we can always choose whose children we want to be. For him, Cato, the towering, resolute Stoic who railed against Julius Caesar in defense of the Republic, was always standing by in his mind. The first book in Marcus Aurelius's *Meditations* is a catalog of all the people he had learned from and the lessons he had taken from their lives. Use this week to think of models that you can follow, wise and admirable people you can measure yourself against.

"We like to say that we don't get to choose our parents, that they were given by chance—yet we can truly choose whose children we'd like to be."

—SENECA, *ON THE BREVITY OF LIFE*, 15.3A

"We can remove most sins if we have a witness standing by as we are about to go wrong. The soul should have someone it can respect, by whose example it can make its inner sanctum more inviolable. Happy is the person who can improve others, not only when present, but even when in their thoughts!"

—SENECA, *MORAL LETTERS*, 11.9

June 4th   Do I realize how tough and strong I am capable of being?

MORNING REFLECTION

EVENING REFLECTION

June 5th   Can I blow my own nose—instead of asking someone to do it for me?

MORNING REFLECTION

EVENING REFLECTION

June 6th　Is this a time to stick or to quit?

MORNING REFLECTION

EVENING REFLECTION

June 7th   What mentors do I follow—alive or dead?

MORNING REFLECTION

EVENING REFLECTION

June 8th   If I took things patiently, step by step, what could I conquer?

MORNING REFLECTION

EVENING REFLECTION

June 9th   What do I need to nip in the bud right now?

MORNING REFLECTION

EVENING REFLECTION

June 10th   If someone else was strong enough to do it, why can't I?

MORNING REFLECTION

EVENING REFLECTION

WEEK XXIV
TRY THE OTHER HANDLE

Epictetus offered a powerful tool in his handbook, the *Enchiridion*, which Stoics use as an exercise in decision-making about difficult events. Everything, Epictetus said, has two interpretations, or handles by which they can be grabbed: one that will make it harder, one that will make it easier. Do you take offense? Or do you focus on common ground? Do you focus on all that has gone wrong? Or what has gone right? Ask yourself these questions about everything you see and feel this week. Make sure you are using the right handle.

> "Every event has two handles—one by which it can be carried, and one by which it can't. If your brother does you wrong, don't grab it by his wronging, because this is the handle incapable of lifting it. Instead, use the other—that he is your brother, that you were raised together, and then you will have hold of the handle that carries."
>
> —EPICTETUS, *ENCHIRIDION*, 43

> "No, it is events that give rise to fear—when another has power over them or can prevent them, that person becomes able to inspire fear. How is the fortress destroyed? Not by iron or fire, but by judgments . . . here is where we must begin, and it is from this front that we must seize the fortress and throw out the tyrants."
>
> —EPICTETUS, *DISCOURSES*, 4.1.85–86; 87A

June 11th   How often is anger more destructive than what caused it?

MORNING REFLECTION

EVENING REFLECTION

June 12th   Am I learning to be adaptable?

MORNING REFLECTION

EVENING REFLECTION

June 13th   Am I fulfilling my post in this campaign of life, or sleeping on duty?

MORNING REFLECTION

EVENING REFLECTION

June 14th   Do I have a hold on the right handle of this situation?

MORNING REFLECTION

EVENING REFLECTION

June 15th   Can I listen more and talk less today?

MORNING REFLECTION

EVENING REFLECTION

June 16th   Where do I need help? Who can I ask for it?

MORNING REFLECTION

EVENING REFLECTION

June 17th   What am I blaming on chance or luck that's really on me?

MORNING REFLECTION

EVENING REFLECTION

WEEK XXV
TAKE A WALK

Seneca believed we should take frequent wandering walks, because constant work will fracture our minds. (As a writer he must have agreed with the novelist Helen Dunmore, "A problem with a piece of writing often clarifies itself if you go for a long walk.") Take some good walks this week and watch the dullness and feebleness depart. Enjoy the scenery, enjoy being away from your work. Make them part of your morning and evening writing routine. Return with a stimulated mind that's ready to journal about and follow the philosophy you know. You think that it's taking a "break," but really you end up smarter and clearer than you were when you left.

"We should take wandering outdoor walks, so that the mind might be nourished and refreshed by the open air and deep breathing."
—SENECA, *ON TRANQUILITY OF MIND*, 17.8

"Pass through this brief patch of time in harmony with nature, and come to your final resting place gracefully, just as a ripened olive might drop, praising the earth that nourished it and grateful to the tree that gave it growth."
—MARCUS AURELIUS, *MEDITATIONS*, 4.48.2

"The mind must be given relaxation—it will rise improved and sharper after a good break. Just as rich fields must not be forced—for they will quickly lose their fertility if never given a break—so constant work on the anvil will fracture the force of the mind. But it regains its powers if it is set free and relaxed for a while. Constant work gives rise to a certain kind of dullness and feebleness in the rational soul."
—SENECA, *ON TRANQUILITY OF MIND*, 17.5

June 18th Am I ready and able?

MORNING REFLECTION

EVENING REFLECTION

June 19th How can I better keep myself in the present moment?

MORNING REFLECTION

EVENING REFLECTION

June 20th   Am I the calm one in the room or the one who needs to be calmed?

MORNING REFLECTION

EVENING REFLECTION

June 21st   How can I refresh my mind today?

MORNING REFLECTION

EVENING REFLECTION

June 22nd   Am I actually learning from my failures?

MORNING REFLECTION

EVENING REFLECTION

June 23rd   Where am I standing in my own way?

MORNING REFLECTION

EVENING REFLECTION

June 24th Do I really need to argue and quarrel so much?

MORNING REFLECTION

EVENING REFLECTION

WEEK XXVI
WHAT'S IN YOUR WAY *IS* THE WAY

Obstacles are a fact of life. Even the most powerful and lucky of us are not exempt from this reality, but we have a superpower at our hands through Stoic philosophy in that our purposes, intentions, and attitudes can adapt to any conditions to find a way forward. The Stoics had a word for this, *hupexhairesis*, meaning acting with a kind of "reserve-clause" or "reverse-clause" that allows us to reconsider and set a new course of action as needed. Marcus Aurelius tells us that any obstacle can actually become the raw material for a new purpose! How might the obstacles you're facing reveal a new path?

"While it's true that someone can impede our actions, they can't impede our intentions and our attitudes, which have the power of being conditional and adaptable. For the mind adapts and converts any obstacle to its action into a means of achieving it. That which is an impediment to action is turned to advance action. The obstacle on the path becomes the way."

—MARCUS AURELIUS, *MEDITATIONS*, 5.20

". . . just as nature turns to its own purpose any obstacle or any opposition, sets its place in the destined order, and co-opts it, so every rational person can convert any obstacle into the raw material for their own purpose."

—MARCUS AURELIUS, *MEDITATIONS*, 8.35

"You must build up your life action by action, and be content if each one achieves its goal as far as possible—and no one can keep you from this. But there will be some external obstacle! Perhaps, but no obstacle to acting with justice, self-control, and wisdom. But what if some other area of my action is thwarted? Well, gladly accept the obstacle for what it is and shift your attention to what is given, and another action will immediately take its place, one that better fits the life you are building."

—MARCUS AURELIUS, *MEDITATIONS*, 8.32

June 25th   Am I expecting the possible, and not just what I *want*?

MORNING REFLECTION

EVENING REFLECTION

June 26th   What thing do I always do that fails and what if I tried the opposite?

MORNING REFLECTION

EVENING REFLECTION

June 27th   What can this adversity show me?

MORNING REFLECTION

EVENING REFLECTION

June 28th   What can I stop beating myself up over?

MORNING REFLECTION

EVENING REFLECTION

June 29th   What can I stop making excuses for?

MORNING REFLECTION

EVENING REFLECTION

June 30th   How can I use this obstacle as an opportunity?

MORNING REFLECTION

EVENING REFLECTION

July 1st   As a Stoic, what is my job?

MORNING REFLECTION

EVENING REFLECTION

WEEK XXVII
PROTECT YOUR OWN GOOD

Musonius Rufus, one of Epictetus's teachers, taught that human beings are all born with an innate goodness, or, as he put it, with an inclination to virtue. It's our choices that decide whether that goodness comes out or not. We're not bad people, essentially, though we might sometimes do bad things. The purpose of Stoicism then is to remind us of that goodness and to help us work hard to protect it. Spend some time writing about the choices you can make this week—the actions you can take—to do just that.

> "Protect your own good in all that you do, and as concerns everything else take what is given as far as you can make reasoned use of it. If you don't, you'll be unlucky, prone to failure, hindered, and stymied."
>
> —EPICTETUS, *DISCOURSES*, 4.3.11

> "Dig deep within yourself, for there is a fountain of goodness ever ready to flow if you will keep digging."
>
> —MARCUS AURELIUS, *MEDITATIONS*, 7.59

July 2nd   What is the harder choice I'm avoiding?

MORNING REFLECTION

EVENING REFLECTION

July 3rd   What if I saw opportunities instead of obligation?

MORNING REFLECTION

EVENING REFLECTION

July 4th Am I keeping the flame of virtue burning?

MORNING REFLECTION

EVENING REFLECTION

July 5th   Am I doing the honorable thing?

MORNING REFLECTION

EVENING REFLECTION

July 6th   Am I dragging my feet or am I doing my job as a human being?

MORNING REFLECTION

EVENING REFLECTION

July 7th   Can I show Odysseus-like determination and perseverance?

MORNING REFLECTION

EVENING REFLECTION

July 8th   What painful things can I take responsibility for?

MORNING REFLECTION

EVENING REFLECTION

WEEK XXVIII
DON'T LOOK FOR THE THIRD THING

The Stoics teach us that doing well is its own reward. To do the right thing, and to see someone helped by it, is enough. To go around expecting thanks—what Marcus Aurelius described as the "third thing"—on top of it? That's being greedy. Keeping score not only misses the purpose of being good, it's foolish. It sets you up for disappointment. If you are going to do some accounting, look at it from the other direction. How many people have helped us—and what do we owe them in return? Think about clearing your debts this week, and consider forgiving any notion of others owing you.

"One person, on doing well by others, immediately accounts the expected favor in return. Another is not so quick, but still considers the person a debtor and knows the favor. A third kind of person acts as if not conscious of the deed, rather like a vine producing a cluster of grapes without making further demands, like a horse after its race, or a dog after its walk, or a bee after making its honey. Such a person, having done a good deed, won't go shouting from rooftops but simply moves on to the next deed just like the vine produces another bunch of grapes in the right season."

—MARCUS AURELIUS, *MEDITATIONS*, 5.6

"When you've done well and another has benefited by it, why like a fool do you look for a third thing on top—credit for the good deed or a favor in return?"

—MARCUS AURELIUS, *MEDITATIONS*, 7.73

July 9th   Am I on the philosopher's path or winging it?

MORNING REFLECTION

EVENING REFLECTION

July 10th   Am I dedicated to my craft?

MORNING REFLECTION

EVENING REFLECTION

July 11th   How will I improve myself today?

MORNING REFLECTION

EVENING REFLECTION

July 12th   What principles govern my behavior?

MORNING REFLECTION

EVENING REFLECTION

July 13th   Am I ready to be a leader? Ready to do my job?

MORNING REFLECTION

EVENING REFLECTION

July 14th   Am I becoming more humble or less humble?

MORNING REFLECTION

EVENING REFLECTION

July 15th   Can I do the right thing—even without the promise of rewards?

MORNING REFLECTION

EVENING REFLECTION

WEEK XXIX
PRACTICE GENTLENESS INSTEAD OF ANGER

It's easy to imagine Marcus Aurelius losing his temper. His responsibilities were vast and his job required him to work with many frustrating, difficult people. As such, he had an acute sense of the problem of anger, knowing just how counterproductive it can be and how miserable it can make its users. He often repeated a simple exercise designed to preserve goodwill for others by simply replacing anger with gentleness. We can't allow ourselves to desert our goodwill, and we must remind ourselves that no one makes a mistake willingly. Each time you feel anger this week, remember Marcus and see how you might replace it with gentleness—and write these examples down.

"As you move forward along the path of reason, people will stand in your way. They will never be able to keep you from doing what's sound, so don't let them knock out your goodwill for them. Keep a steady watch on both fronts, not only for well-based judgments and actions, but also for gentleness with those who would obstruct our path or create other difficulties. For getting angry is also a weakness, just as much as abandoning the task or surrendering under panic."

—MARCUS AURELIUS, *MEDITATIONS*, 11.9

"As Plato said, every soul is deprived of truth against its will. The same holds true for justice, self-control, goodwill to others, and every similar virtue. It's essential to constantly keep this in your mind, for it will make you more gentle to all."

—MARCUS AURELIUS, *MEDITATIONS*, 7.63

"Keep this thought handy when you feel a fit of rage coming on— it isn't manly to be enraged. Rather, gentleness and civility are more human, and therefore manlier. A real man doesn't give way to anger and discontent, and such a person has strength, courage, and endurance. . . ."

—MARCUS AURELIUS, *MEDITATIONS*, 11.18.5B

July 16th   To what service am I committed?

MORNING REFLECTION

EVENING REFLECTION

July 17th   Where have I abandoned others?

MORNING REFLECTION

EVENING REFLECTION

July 18th   Can I mind my own business and not be distracted by others?

MORNING REFLECTION

EVENING REFLECTION

July 19th   What would forgiveness feel like?

MORNING REFLECTION

EVENING REFLECTION

July 20th   Am I living a just life?

MORNING REFLECTION

EVENING REFLECTION

July 21st   How can I work better with others?

MORNING REFLECTION

EVENING REFLECTION

July 22nd   Am I acting nobly or grudgingly?

MORNING REFLECTION

EVENING REFLECTION

WEEK XXX
KEEPING "THE NEWS" IN CHECK

Even the ancients felt inundated with gossip and news. This week you will face a barrage like they couldn't have imagined—from texts, calls, e-mails to the incessant grind of the 24/7 news machine. Instead of responding to every status update, urgent call, or the latest trending incendiary news story, take a moment to remember three ways the Stoics used to keep their focus on their purpose and duty in the present moment: (1) Step away from the noise. (2) Remember that no news can throw you off the purpose of your present choices. (3) Don't add something negative (or positive) to what is being reported.

"Are you distracted by breaking news? Then take some leisure time to learn something good, and stop bouncing around. But when you do, keep in mind the other mistake, to be so distracted by getting control that you wear yourself out and lose a purpose by which you can direct your impulses and thoughts."

—Marcus Aurelius, *Meditations*, 2.7

"Whenever disturbing news is delivered to you, bear in mind that *no news can ever be relevant to your reasoned choice*. Can anyone break news to you that your assumptions or desires are wrong? No way! But they can tell you someone died—even so, what is that to you?"

—Epictetus, *Discourses*, 3.18.1–2

"*Don't tell yourself anything more than what the initial impressions report.* It's been reported to you that someone is speaking badly about you. This is the report—the report wasn't that you've been harmed. I see that my son is sick—but not that his life is at risk. So always stay within your first impressions, and don't add to them in your head—this way nothing can happen to you."

—Marcus Aurelius, *Meditations*, 8.49

July 23rd   How can I make sure none of it goes to my head—good or bad?

MORNING REFLECTION

EVENING REFLECTION

July 24th   Can I keep my cool when receiving disturbing news?

MORNING REFLECTION

EVENING REFLECTION

July 25th   Where do I let work diminish my quality of life?

MORNING REFLECTION

EVENING REFLECTION

July 26th   Where can I pitch in? How can I help?

MORNING REFLECTION

EVENING REFLECTION

July 27th   What is better than virtue?

MORNING REFLECTION

EVENING REFLECTION

July 28th   Where have I been privileged—and what am I doing with it?

MORNING REFLECTION

EVENING REFLECTION

July 29th   Where can I find confidence?

MORNING REFLECTION

EVENING REFLECTION

WEEK XXXI
A WEEK WITHOUT COMPLAINING

Epictetus spoke often to his students about the need to give up blaming and complaining—in fact, he saw it as one of the primary measuring sticks of progress in the art of living. How much of life is wasted pointing fingers? Has complaining ever solved a single problem? Marcus Aurelius would say, "Blame yourself—or no one." This week, try constructive feedback over complaining and responsibility over blame. And if something goes wrong, spend some time reflecting on what the true causes were. Don't waste a minute with complaints—in this journal or out loud.

> "You must stop blaming God, and not blame any person. You must completely control your desire and shift your avoidance to what lies within your reasoned choice. You must no longer feel anger, resentment, envy, or regret."
>
> —Epictetus, *Discourses*, 3.22.13

> "For nothing outside my reasoned choice can hinder or harm it— my reasoned choice alone can do this to itself. If we would lean this way whenever we fail, and would blame only ourselves and remember that nothing but opinion is the cause of a troubled mind and uneasiness, then by God, I swear we would be making progress."
>
> —Epictetus, *Discourses*, 3.19.2–3

> "But if you deem as your own only what is yours, and what belongs to others as truly not yours, then no one will ever be able to coerce or to stop you, you will find no one to blame or accuse, you will do nothing against your will, you will have no enemy, no one will harm you, because no harm can affect you."
>
> —Epictetus, *Enchiridion*, 1.3

July 30th Can I seek joy today in purpose, excellence, and duty?

MORNING REFLECTION

EVENING REFLECTION

July 31st Am I neglecting the personal for the professional?

MORNING REFLECTION

EVENING REFLECTION

August 1st   Where does my idealism hold me back?

MORNING REFLECTION

EVENING REFLECTION

August 2nd   How can I make do with the tough situations I face?

MORNING REFLECTION

EVENING REFLECTION

August 3rd   Can I get the most out of where I am right here, right now?

MORNING REFLECTION

EVENING REFLECTION

August 4th　How can I avoid fruitless emotions today?

MORNING REFLECTION

EVENING REFLECTION

August 5th   Can I hold my tongue today?

MORNING REFLECTION

EVENING REFLECTION

WEEK XXXII
WHAT LITTLE WINS CAN YOU FIND?

Zeno of Citium, the Phoenician merchant who founded the Stoic school on the painted porch (*stoa poikilē*) of the Agora after a shipwreck, said that happiness was a matter of small steps. While the Stoics believed in the perfectibility of human beings, they knew much stood in the way of realizing that potential. So they would be skeptical of the so-called epic wins and quantum leaps that our culture obsesses over today. Instead, they would urge you to focus on your daily duties, on making incremental progress. Spend your writing time this week thinking about the small wins you can rack up, what little gains can be had from this improvement or that one, a decision here or a decision there. Be satisfied with each small step. Keep moving and don't give up.

"Do now what nature demands of you. Get right to it if that's in your power. Don't look around to see if people will know about it. Don't await the perfection of Plato's *Republic*, but be satisfied with even the smallest step forward and regard the outcome as a small thing."

—MARCUS AURELIUS, *MEDITATIONS*, 9.29

"We don't abandon our pursuits because we despair of ever perfecting them."

—EPICTETUS, *DISCOURSES*, 1.2.37B

"Well-being is realized by small steps, but is truly no small thing."

—ZENO, QUOTED IN DIOGENES LAERTIUS, *LIVES OF THE EMINENT PHILOSOPHERS*, 7.1.26

August 6th   Do I think through my problems to apply the right pressure?

MORNING REFLECTION

EVENING REFLECTION

August 7th   Can I live well no matter how trying the environment?

MORNING REFLECTION

EVENING REFLECTION

August 8th　What's the smallest step I can take toward a big thing today?

MORNING REFLECTION

EVENING REFLECTION

August 9th   Can I keep things simple today? Straightforward?

MORNING REFLECTION

EVENING REFLECTION

August 10th   Where is perfectionism holding me back?

MORNING REFLECTION

EVENING REFLECTION

August 11th   Are my habits getting better?

MORNING REFLECTION

EVENING REFLECTION

August 12th   Am I making this philosophy my own by putting it into practice?

MORNING REFLECTION

EVENING REFLECTION

WEEK XXXIII
ALWAYS ASK YOURSELF THIS QUESTION

Much of what we do and say during the course of a week is completely unnecessary. Meetings, material possessions, confrontations, pursuits—pointless distractions and problems. They take us away from tranquility and purpose. A Stoic cuts through these temptations and obligations by asking this question, a question that you should lead your journaling with this week. Try it. Before speaking, acting, or buying something, ask simply: "Is this one of the necessary things?"

"It is said that if you would have peace of mind, busy yourself with little. But wouldn't a better saying be do what you must and as required of a rational being created for public life? For this brings not only the peace of mind of doing few things, but the greater peace of doing them well. Since the vast majority of our words and actions are unnecessary, corralling them will create an abundance of leisure and tranquility. As a result, we shouldn't forget at each moment to ask, is this one of the unnecessary things? But we must corral not only unnecessary actions but unnecessary thoughts, too, so needless acts don't tag along after them."
—MARCUS AURELIUS, *MEDITATIONS*, 4.24

"I was shipwrecked before I even boarded . . . the journey showed me this—how much of what we have is unnecessary, and how easily we can decide to rid ourselves of these things whenever it's necessary, never suffering the loss."
—SENECA, *MORAL LETTERS*, 87.1

August 13th   What troubles can I solve in advance?

MORNING REFLECTION

EVENING REFLECTION

August 14th   How will philosophy help steer my course today?

MORNING REFLECTION

EVENING REFLECTION

August 15th   Will decisions I make today be based on true judgments?

MORNING REFLECTION

EVENING REFLECTION

August 16th   How will I turn today's adversities into advantages?

MORNING REFLECTION

EVENING REFLECTION

August 17th   Can I go a whole day without blaming others?

MORNING REFLECTION

EVENING REFLECTION

August 18th   Where can I better play to my strengths?

MORNING REFLECTION

EVENING REFLECTION

August 19th   What inessential things can I eliminate from my life?

MORNING REFLECTION

EVENING REFLECTION

WEEK XXXIV

JUST SAY NO TO FUTURE MISERY

How often we make ourselves miserable . . . in advance. Out of fear of this, out of desperate hope for that. When we focus on pining for or avoiding a certain future, we make ourselves miserable here in the present. Hecato of Rhodes, the great student of the great middle-Stoic scholar Panaetius, taught that this misery is always tied to hopes or fears we give to imagined future outcomes. From this Seneca reminds us this week to say no to both, because indulging them robs us of the ability to enjoy the present. As you write, don't think about the future—what you hope will happen, what you fear might—just focus on right now. What you're doing and thinking right now.

"It's ruinous for the soul to be anxious about the future and miserable in advance of misery, engulfed by anxiety that the things it desires might remain its own until the very end. For such a soul will never be at rest—by longing for things to come it will lose the ability to enjoy present things."

—SENECA, *MORAL LETTERS*, 98.5B–6A

"But there is no reason to live and no limit to our miseries if we let our fears predominate."

—SENECA, *MORAL LETTERS*, 13.12B

"Hecato says, 'Cease to hope and you will cease to fear.'. . . The primary cause of both these ills is that instead of adapting ourselves to present circumstances we send out thoughts too far ahead."

—SENECA, *MORAL LETTERS*, 5.7B–8

August 20th   How well is my soul dressed?

MORNING REFLECTION

EVENING REFLECTION

August 21st   What if I stopped worrying about the future and enjoyed the present?

MORNING REFLECTION

EVENING REFLECTION

August 22nd   What small stuff can I stop sweating?

MORNING REFLECTION

EVENING REFLECTION

August 23rd   Where do I have too much of a good thing?

MORNING REFLECTION

EVENING REFLECTION

August 24th   What can I learn from others—even the people I don't like?

MORNING REFLECTION

EVENING REFLECTION

August 25th What new path can I blaze today?

MORNING REFLECTION

EVENING REFLECTION

August 26th   What potential losses can I anticipate in advance?

MORNING REFLECTION

EVENING REFLECTION

WEEK XXXV
A CURE FOR PROCRASTINATION

To the Stoic, procrastination almost looks like a form of delusion and entitlement. Who is to say you'll even be around next month or next week to deal with it? If it's important, they'd say, don't wait. Do it now. As Seneca says, if it needs to be done, do it with "courage and promptness." Procrastination seems like it makes things easier, but it damns us to a low-grade, gnawing state of anxiety. Is that how you'd want to spend this week? Any week? Your last week? Ask yourself: What am I avoiding? What can I handle today instead of tomorrow? What can I do promptly and bravely, right now?

> "Anything that must yet be done, virtue can do with courage and promptness. For anyone would call it a sign of foolishness for one to undertake a task with a lazy and begrudging spirit, or to push the body in one direction and the mind in another, to be torn apart by wildly divergent impulses."
>
> —SENECA, *MORAL LETTERS*, 74.31B–32

> "This is the mark of perfection of character—to spend each day as if it were your last, without frenzy, laziness, or any pretending."
>
> —MARCUS AURELIUS, *MEDITATIONS*, 7.69

> "You get what you deserve. Instead of being a good person today, you choose instead to become one tomorrow."
>
> —MARCUS AURELIUS, *MEDITATIONS*, 8.22

August 27th   Where can I learn to laugh rather than cry?

MORNING REFLECTION

EVENING REFLECTION

August 28th   What luxuries can I practice not needing?

MORNING REFLECTION

EVENING REFLECTION

August 29th What wants can I eliminate today?

MORNING REFLECTION

EVENING REFLECTION

August 30th   Can I do today's duties with both courage and confidence?

MORNING REFLECTION

EVENING REFLECTION

August 31st   Where have I done others wrong?

MORNING REFLECTION

EVENING REFLECTION

September 1st   Am I working to make my soul stronger than any Fortune?

MORNING REFLECTION

EVENING REFLECTION

September 2nd   What's the most painful part of Stoicism for you?

MORNING REFLECTION

EVENING REFLECTION

WEEK XXXVI
A HARD WINTER TRAINING

The art of living has three levels of discipline: study, practice, and hard training. Reading the Stoics, that's study. Trying out the lessons and reflecting on them in this journal, that's practice. What's left is the hard training. Epictetus liked to use the analogy of the Roman army's practice of training hard in the off months of winter so they would be prepared to meet any challenge when they returned to battle in the spring. Seneca would spend time each month exposing himself to tougher than usual conditions. He, too, used a military analogy, pointing to the way soldiers are tasked with hard jobs so they would be strong when the enemy eventually came. What are you doing this week to push yourself beyond mere study and practice?

"We must undergo a hard winter training and not rush into things for which we haven't prepared."

—EPICTETUS, *DISCOURSES*, 1.2.32

"Here's a lesson to test your mind's mettle: take part of a week in which you have only the most meager and cheap food, dress scantly in shabby clothes, and ask yourself if this is really the worst that you feared. It is when times are good that you should gird yourself for tougher times ahead, for when Fortune is kind the soul can build defenses against her ravages. So it is that soldiers practice maneuvers in peacetime, erecting bunkers with no enemies in sight and exhausting themselves under no attack so that when it comes they won't grow tired."

—SENECA, *MORAL LETTERS*, 18.5–6

"When a challenge confronts you, remember that God is matching you with a younger sparring partner, as would a physical trainer. Why? Becoming an Olympian takes sweat! I think no one has a better challenge than yours, if only you would use it like an athlete would that younger sparring partner."

—EPICTETUS, *DISCOURSES*, 1.24.1–2

September 3rd   How am I preparing in the off-season for what is to come?

MORNING REFLECTION

EVENING REFLECTION

September 4th   How can I see these difficulties as a lesson and a test?

MORNING REFLECTION

EVENING REFLECTION

September 5th   What is truly mine?

MORNING REFLECTION

EVENING REFLECTION

September 6th   If I lost my freedom, would it break me?

MORNING REFLECTION

EVENING REFLECTION

September 7th   How will I use the power of choice today?

MORNING REFLECTION

EVENING REFLECTION

September 8th   Am I prepared for my bubble to be burst?

MORNING REFLECTION

EVENING REFLECTION

September 9th   Do I rule my fears, or do they rule me?

MORNING REFLECTION

EVENING REFLECTION

WEEK XXXVII
A NEW WAY TO PRAY

We often pray for the things we desire and, in the process, excuse ourselves from the equation. We're hoping the heavens will magically gift us with the outcome we want—whether it's for a promotion or the speedy recovery of a loved one. The Stoics would urge you to stop doing this. Marcus Aurelius reminded himself not to present the gods with a list of demands for pleasures or comforts, but instead to ask for help not needing those things. In a sense then, he was really asking for inner strength. He was asking *himself*. Think about all the things you want—that you're praying or hoping for this week—and try turning them around like that. See what you come up with instead.

> "Try praying differently, and see what happens: Instead of asking for 'a way to sleep with her,' try asking for 'a way to stop desiring to sleep with her.' Instead of 'a way to get rid of him,' try asking for 'a way to not crave his demise.' Instead of 'a way to not lose my child,' try asking for 'a way to lose my fear of it.'"
>
> —MARCUS AURELIUS, *MEDITATIONS*, 9.40.(6)

> "We cry to God Almighty, how can we escape this agony? Fool, don't you have hands? Or could it be God forgot to give you a pair? Sit and pray your nose doesn't run! Or rather just wipe your nose and stop seeking a scapegoat."
>
> —EPICTETUS, *DISCOURSES*, 2.16.13

> "But I haven't at any time been hindered in my will, nor forced against it. And how is this possible? I have bound up my choice to act with the will of God. God wills that I be sick, such is my will. He wills that I should choose something, so do I. He wills that I reach for something, or something be given to me—I wish for the same. What God doesn't will, I do not wish for."
>
> —EPICTETUS, *DISCOURSES*, 4.1.89

September 10th How can I prepare for the losses I fear?

MORNING REFLECTION

EVENING REFLECTION

September 11th Where can I do with less today?

MORNING REFLECTION

EVENING REFLECTION

September 12th Where am I putting on airs?

MORNING REFLECTION

EVENING REFLECTION

September 13th   How strong is my Inner Citadel?

MORNING REFLECTION

EVENING REFLECTION

September 14th   Are you praying—or *demanding*?

MORNING REFLECTION

EVENING REFLECTION

September 15th　Are you sizzle or steak?

MORNING REFLECTION

EVENING REFLECTION

September 16th   Will I triumph over the disasters and panics of the day?

MORNING REFLECTION

EVENING REFLECTION

WEEK XXXVIII
ON HANDLING HATERS

The Stoics taught that kindness trumps hate. They believed that those who engage in hate are prisoners to a destructive passion—one that hurts the practitioner, not the intended target. There's no reason to hate a hater; they are already suffering enough. In fact, when you see them this way, it makes it easier to be kind, good-natured, genuine, and useful. Remember the line in the Bible about how loving your enemies is like pouring hot coals on them, because it's so unexpected? Who can you surprise like that this week? Whose enmity can you meet with kindness and compassion? How much better do you feel having done so?

"What if someone despises me? Let them see to it. But I will see to it that I won't be found doing or saying anything contemptible. What if someone hates me? Let them see to that. But I will see to it that I'm kind and good-natured to all, and prepared to show even the hater where they went wrong. Not in a critical way, or to show off my patience, but genuinely and usefully."

—MARCUS AURELIUS, *MEDITATIONS*, 11.13

"Kindness is invincible, but only when it's sincere, with no hypocrisy or faking. For what can even the most malicious person do if you keep showing kindness and, if given the chance, you gently point out where they went wrong—right as they are trying to harm you?"

—MARCUS AURELIUS, *MEDITATIONS*, 11.18.5.9a

"Keep in mind that it isn't the one who has it in for you and takes a swipe that harms you, but rather the harm comes from your own belief about the abuse. So when someone arouses your anger, know that it's really your own opinion fueling it. Instead, make it your first response not to be carried away by such impressions, for with time and distance self-mastery is more easily achieved."

—EPICTETUS, *ENCHIRIDION*, 20

September 17th   Can I resist giving in to haters—and hating them in return?

MORNING REFLECTION

EVENING REFLECTION

September 18th   Can I let the pains of life pass without adding to them?

MORNING REFLECTION

EVENING REFLECTION

September 19th　Am I flexible enough to change my mind and accept feedback?

MORNING REFLECTION

EVENING REFLECTION

September 20th   How ready am I for unexpected attacks?

MORNING REFLECTION

EVENING REFLECTION

September 21st   Can I keep life's rhythm no matter the interruption?

MORNING REFLECTION

EVENING REFLECTION

September 22nd   How will today's difficulties show my character?

MORNING REFLECTION

EVENING REFLECTION

September 23rd   How is my training coming?

MORNING REFLECTION

EVENING REFLECTION

WEEK XXXIX
PANIC IS SELF-INFLICTED HARM

Name one situation that is improved by panicking. Go ahead—write it down if you've got one! Seneca mused often about the problem of panic both in his letters and essays. It creates danger and limits our ability to function effectively. It prevents us from finding success and seeing objectively. Worse, it makes us weaker over time because we've never truly faced the danger we are so worried about. Meditate on the scary things that might make you panic. Think about what is so overwhelming about them. Come to understand them. Get familiar with them.

> "For even peace itself will supply more reason for worry. Not even safe circumstances will bring you confidence once your mind has been shocked—once it gets in the habit of blind panic, it can't provide for its own safety. For it doesn't really avoid danger, it just runs away. Yet we are exposed to greater danger with our backs turned."
>
> —SENECA, *MORAL LETTERS*, 104.10b

> "Success comes to the lowly and to the poorly talented, but the special characteristic of a great person is to triumph over the disasters and panics of human life."
>
> —SENECA, *ON PROVIDENCE*, 4.1

> "The unprepared are panic-stricken by the smallest things."
>
> —SENECA, *MORAL LETTERS*, 107.4

September 24th   Have I thought about *all* that might happen?

MORNING REFLECTION

EVENING REFLECTION

September 25th   What am I a slave to?

MORNING REFLECTION

After morning cabinet meeting

EVENING REFLECTION

September 26th   What idle leisure can I replace with something more fulfilling?

MORNING REFLECTION

EVENING REFLECTION

September 27th   What do prosperity and difficulty each reveal about me?

MORNING REFLECTION

EVENING REFLECTION

September 28th   How will I respond to the things that happen today?

MORNING REFLECTION

EVENING REFLECTION

September 29th   Where are my eyes bigger than my stomach?

MORNING REFLECTION

EVENING REFLECTION

September 30th   How can I strengthen my Inner Citadel?

MORNING REFLECTION

EVENING REFLECTION

WEEK XL
PRACTICE SILENCE

Social media teaches us to have an opinion about everything. Silence beckons us to speak. We live in a loud culture and we try to keep up by being louder in return. How much trouble does that cause us? How much might we learn if we spent more time listening to others than we do trying to sandwich our opinions in at every turn? How much of what we say have we come to regret? The truly loud thing to say is nothing. Write your thoughts down here this week, but see how many of them you can keep to yourself. Be bold in your silence, in how much you hold your tongue this week.

"Better to trip with the feet than with the tongue."
—Zeno, Quoted in Diogenes Laertius,
Lives of the Eminent Philosophers, 7.1.26

"To the youngster talking nonsense Zeno said, 'The reason why we have two ears and only one mouth is so we might listen more and talk less.'"
—Diogenes Laertius,
Lives of the Eminent Philosophers, 7.1.23

"Cato practiced the kind of public speech capable of moving the masses, believing proper political philosophy takes care like any great city to maintain the warlike element. But he was never seen practicing in front of others, and no one ever heard him rehearse a speech. When he was told that people blamed him for his silence, he replied, 'Better they not blame my life. I begin to speak only when I'm certain what I'll say isn't better left unsaid.'"
—Plutarch, *Cato the Younger*, 4

"Silence is a lesson learned from the many sufferings of life."
—Seneca, *Thyestes*, 309

October 1st   How will I let my virtues shine today?

MORNING REFLECTION

EVENING REFLECTION

October 2nd   If wisdom is the most valuable asset, how have I invested in it?

MORNING REFLECTION

EVENING REFLECTION

October 3rd   Do I live as if we are all one—all part of the same whole?

MORNING REFLECTION

EVENING REFLECTION

October 4th   Will my actions today be good for all concerned?

MORNING REFLECTION

EVENING REFLECTION

October 5th   What do I say that's better left unsaid?

MORNING REFLECTION

EVENING REFLECTION

October 6th   Who else can I root for—other than myself?

MORNING REFLECTION

EVENING REFLECTION

October 7th   Why does my wrongdoing hurt me most of all?

MORNING REFLECTION

EVENING REFLECTION

WEEK XLI
PRACTICE LOVE

The Stoic notion of *sympatheia*, that we all are part of an organic whole, connected by mutual interests and affinities, is greater than the Golden Rule. Don't treat others how you would like to be treated, treat them like you treat yourself, because we are all one. Seneca said that whenever he encountered another human being he saw an opportunity for kindness. He had learned from Hecato that if you want to be loved there is only one thing to do: love others. Who can you give love to this week? What kindness can you expend? How can you show how you feel—strangers, friends, and family? How can you show them that you believe we are all part of the same whole?

"Hecato says, 'I can teach you a love potion made without any drugs, herbs, or special spell—if you would be loved, love.'"
—SENECA, *MORAL LETTERS*, 9.6

"A benefit should be kept like a buried treasure, only to be dug up in necessity. . . . Nature bids us to do well by all. . . . Wherever there is a human being, we have an opportunity for kindness."
—SENECA, *ON THE HAPPY LIFE*, 24.2–3

"Nature produced us as a family, since we all sprang from the same source and toward the same end. Nature bestowed upon us mutual love, and joined us together as friends."
—SENECA, *MORAL LETTERS*, 95.52

October 8th   What is more pleasing than wisdom?

MORNING REFLECTION

EVENING REFLECTION

October 9th   Have I set my standards and am I using them?

MORNING REFLECTION

EVENING REFLECTION

October 10th   What do my principles tell me about persisting and resisting?

MORNING REFLECTION

EVENING REFLECTION

October 11th   Is honesty my default setting?

MORNING REFLECTION

EVENING REFLECTION

October 12th   Instead of seeking love can I give it first?

MORNING REFLECTION

EVENING REFLECTION

October 13th   Has revenge ever made anything better?

MORNING REFLECTION

EVENING REFLECTION

October 14th   What if instead of getting mad, I offered to help?

MORNING REFLECTION

EVENING REFLECTION

WEEK XLII

MAKE HONESTY YOUR ONLY POLICY

As emperor, Marcus Aurelius did not see the best of humanity. At court there would have been backbiting, people who sold their friends out when they saw an opportunity to advance themselves, avarice, and deceit. But he especially didn't like faux attempts at honesty. His point: if you have to say "I'm going to be honest with you here," you're casually saying that honesty is the exception and not the rule. How sad is that? It's time to think about what those little statements say about us—and make sure that our default policy is honesty and straightforwardness.

> "How rotten and fraudulent when people say they intend to give it to you straight. What are you up to, dear friend? It shouldn't need your announcement, but be readily seen, as if written on your forehead, heard in the ring of your voice, a flash in your eyes—just as the beloved sees it all in the lover's glance. In short, the straightforward and good person should be like a smelly goat—you know when they are in the room with you. A calculated 'giving it to you straight' is like a dagger. There's nothing worse than a wolf befriending sheep. Avoid false friendship at all costs. If you are good, straightforward, and well-meaning it should show in your eyes and not escape notice."
>
> —MARCUS AURELIUS, *MEDITATIONS*, 11.15

> "It's in keeping with Nature to show our friends affection and to celebrate their advancement, as if it were our very own. For if we don't do this, virtue, which is strengthened only by exercising our perceptions, will no longer endure in us."
>
> —SENECA, *MORAL LETTERS*, 109.15

October 15th   Will I give people the benefit of the doubt?

MORNING REFLECTION

EVENING REFLECTION

October 16th   How can I share this philosophy that has helped me so much?

MORNING REFLECTION

EVENING REFLECTION

October 17th   Where can I show other people kindness?

MORNING REFLECTION

EVENING REFLECTION

October 18th   Am I avoiding false friendships and bad influences?

MORNING REFLECTION

EVENING REFLECTION

October 19th   Which good habit can I use today to drive out a bad one?

MORNING REFLECTION

EVENING REFLECTION

October 20th   Do my principles show themselves in my life?

MORNING REFLECTION

EVENING REFLECTION

October 21st   Can I do the right thing and not care about credit?

MORNING REFLECTION

EVENING REFLECTION

WEEK XLIII
BUILD UP, DON'T TEAR DOWN

Is there a worse environment to work in than one where bullying and one-upmanship is the norm? Sometimes leaders seem to think that that is part of the job description—that they are there to regulate and keep people in line. In truth, tearing people down is incredibly counterproductive. Pete Carroll, coach of the Seattle Seahawks, poses a question: If self-confidence is so important for players, why would a coach ever do anything to damage it? Marcus Aurelius, who had the power to take down anyone at will, almost never did. Instead, he reminded himself that it was better to build up—be community-minded, modest, prepared, and tolerant of others. We are made for cooperation (*synergia*) and to render works held in common (*praxeis koinonikas apodidonai*). Let's think about that going forward: How can we help build the self-confidence of others? How can we find some of our own in doing so?

"So someone's good at taking down an opponent, but that doesn't make them more community-minded, or modest, or well-prepared for any circumstance, or more tolerant of the faults of others."
—MARCUS AURELIUS, *MEDITATIONS*, 7.52

"Whenever you have trouble getting up in the morning, remind yourself that you've been made by nature for the purpose of working with others. . . . And it's our own natural purpose that is more fitting and more satisfying."
—MARCUS AURELIUS, *MEDITATIONS*, 8.12

October 22nd   Am I actually improving—or am I just chasing vanity?

MORNING REFLECTION

EVENING REFLECTION

October 23rd   Am I displaying my best qualities?

MORNING REFLECTION

EVENING REFLECTION

October 24th　What goodness can I find inside myself? Can I bring it to the surface?

MORNING REFLECTION

EVENING REFLECTION

October 25th   What are my tasks in this life?

MORNING REFLECTION

EVENING REFLECTION

October 26th   Are my goals natural, moral, and rational?

MORNING REFLECTION

EVENING REFLECTION

October 27th   What bad behaviors or choices have come back to haunt me?

MORNING REFLECTION

EVENING REFLECTION

October 28th   What can I do to be part of something bigger than myself?

MORNING REFLECTION

EVENING REFLECTION

WEEK XLIV
ACCEPTING WHAT IS

Reinhold Niebuhr's Serenity Prayer is a mantra for many: "God grant me the serenity to accept the things I cannot change; courage to change the things I can; and wisdom to know the difference." The Stoics wanted to push past simply "accepting" what is—they wanted to be grateful and happy with what it is. Epictetus taught that we get a well-flowing life when we wish for what is going to happen not what we want to happen, and Marcus added that we should meet anything that comes our way with gratitude. Not "I wish this was different, but I'll tolerate it"; instead "I am glad it happened this way. It is for the best." Try that on for size this week.

"Don't seek for everything to happen as you wish it would, but rather wish that everything happens as it actually will—then your life will flow well."

—EPICTETUS, *ENCHIRIDION*, 8

"To be truly educated means this—learning to wish that each thing happens exactly as it does."

—EPICTETUS, *DISCOURSES*, 1.12.15

"All you need are these: certainty of judgment in the present moment; action for the common good in the present moment; and an attitude of gratitude in the present moment for anything that comes your way."

—MARCUS AURELIUS, *MEDITATIONS*, 9.6

October 29th   How can I improve my character?

MORNING REFLECTION

EVENING REFLECTION

October 30th   What time can I claw back for myself—and how will I use it?

MORNING REFLECTION

EVENING REFLECTION

October 31st   What good turns can be done today?

MORNING REFLECTION

EVENING REFLECTION

November 1st   Can I love *everything* that happens today?

MORNING REFLECTION

EVENING REFLECTION

November 2nd   Can I make my choices and accept whatever will be?

MORNING REFLECTION

EVENING REFLECTION

November 3rd   How can this be exactly what I needed?

MORNING REFLECTION

EVENING REFLECTION

November 4th   Is change really so bad? Is the status quo really so good?

MORNING REFLECTION

EVENING REFLECTION

∽∞

WEEK XLV
THE REAL POWER YOU HAVE

There is fleeting power and there is real power. Fleeting power can be taken away, while real power is in our minds and our bones. The former tends to be along the lines of wealth, fame, high position, and the leverage all those things give us over others. The Stoics thought this kind of power was inferior to the real power that each person possesses—the power of our minds to reason and make judgments and choices based on the real worth of things. You can have both kinds of power, too, but only if you keep the first kind of power subject to the kind of power the Stoics cared about.

"This is the very thing which makes up the virtue of the happy person and a well-flowing life—when the affairs of life are in every way tuned to the harmony between the individual divine spirit and the will of the director of the universe."

—CHRYSIPPUS, QUOTED IN DIOGENES LAERTIUS,
LIVES OF THE EMINENT PHILOSOPHERS, 7.1.88

"Don't trust in your reputation, money, or position, but in the strength that is yours—namely, your judgments about the things that you control and don't control. For this alone is what makes us free and unfettered, that picks us up by the neck from the depths and lifts us eye to eye with the rich and powerful."

—EPICTETUS, DISCOURSES, 3.26.34–35

"Understand at last that you have something in you more powerful and divine than what causes the bodily passions and pulls you like a mere puppet. What thoughts now occupy my mind? Is it not fear, suspicion, desire, or something like that?"

—MARCUS AURELIUS, MEDITATIONS, 12.19

November 5th   Is my character producing a well-flowing life?

MORNING REFLECTION

EVENING REFLECTION

November 6th   Am I prepared for the randomness of fate and luck?

MORNING REFLECTION

EVENING REFLECTION

November 7th   Are you trying to master yourself—or other people?

MORNING REFLECTION

EVENING REFLECTION

November 8th   What's my role in the play of life?

MORNING REFLECTION

EVENING REFLECTION

November 9th   What principles will steer me through the flow of change?

MORNING REFLECTION

EVENING REFLECTION

November 10th   What will remain when all else passes away?

MORNING REFLECTION

EVENING REFLECTION

November 11th   What false judgment can I wipe away today?

MORNING REFLECTION

EVENING REFLECTION

WEEK XLVI
JUDGE YOURSELF, NOT OTHERS

There is nothing less philosophical than being a know-it-all. This is especially true of those who use their knowledge to scold others for their mistakes while proclaiming the superiority of their knowledge or insight. The Stoics taught that behaving this way was to miss the entire purpose of philosophy—as a tool for self-correction, medicine for our own souls, not a weapon for putting others down. Seneca's letters twice employ the metaphor of scrubbing down or scraping off our faults. We need to see ourselves as "in the care of philosophy's principles," or, as Epictetus put it later when referring to the philosopher's lecture hall, we need to see it as a hospital for our own therapy. Don't let yourself write down a single complaint or problem of another person in this journal this week—focus on what ails you.

"When philosophy is wielded with arrogance and stubbornly, it is the cause for the ruin of many. Let philosophy scrape off your own faults, rather than be a way to rail against the faults of others."
—SENECA, *MORAL LETTERS*, 103.4B–5A

"Some people with exceptional minds quickly grasp virtue or produce it within themselves. But other dim and lazy types, hindered by bad habits, must have their rusty souls constantly scrubbed down. . . . The weaker sorts will be helped and lifted from their bad opinions if we put them in the care of philosophy's principles."
—SENECA, *MORAL LETTERS*, 95.36–37

"Men, the philosopher's lecture-hall is a hospital—you shouldn't walk out of it feeling pleasure, but pain, for you aren't well when you enter it."
—EPICTETUS, *DISCOURSES*, 3.23.30

November 12th   Can the buck stop with me today?

MORNING REFLECTION

EVENING REFLECTION

November 13th   Does complaining accomplish anything?

MORNING REFLECTION

EVENING REFLECTION

November 14th   Will I add negative thoughts on top of my troubles?

MORNING REFLECTION

EVENING REFLECTION

November 15th   Will I embrace the flow of change today?

MORNING REFLECTION

EVENING REFLECTION

November 16th   Can I cease both hoping for and fearing certain outcomes?

MORNING REFLECTION

EVENING REFLECTION

November 17th   Is it really my place to judge other people?

MORNING REFLECTION

EVENING REFLECTION

November 18th   Am I practicing good Stoic thoughts?

MORNING REFLECTION

EVENING REFLECTION

WEEK XLVII
PRACTICE LETTING GO

We suffer when we lose things we love, and we suffer most when we lose people we love—a natural and unavoidable part of life. The Stoics say this suffering is increased by our belief that we possess the objects of our love—that they are, as we like to say, "a part of us." This belief doesn't increase our love and care for them, but rather is a form of clinging that ignores the simple fact that we don't control what will happen, not to our own bodies, let alone to the ones we love. Epictetus taught a powerful exercise that every time you wish a dear child, family member, or friend good night, remember that these people are like a precious breakable glass, and remember how dramatically things could change while you sleep. Marcus, too, struggled to practice this with his own family as he tucked them in at night. The point isn't to be morbid but to create a sense of appreciation and a kind of humility. Don't take anyone—especially someone you love—for granted this week.

"Whenever you experience the pangs of losing something, don't treat it like a part of yourself but as a breakable glass, so when it falls you will remember that and won't be troubled. So, too, whenever you kiss your child, sibling, or friend, don't layer on top of the experience all the things you might wish, but hold them back and stop them, just as those who ride behind triumphant generals remind them they are mortal. In the same way, remind yourself that your precious one isn't one of your possessions, but something given for now, not forever."

—EPICTETUS, *DISCOURSES*, 3.24.84–86A

"But the wise person can lose nothing. Such a person has everything stored up for themselves, leaving nothing to Fortune, their own goods are held firm, bound in virtue, which requires nothing from chance, and therefore can't be either increased or diminished."

—SENECA, *ON THE FIRMNESS OF THE WISE*, 5.4

November 19th   Will I accept the situation and still fight to do and be good?

MORNING REFLECTION

EVENING REFLECTION

November 20th   Where can I find timelessness in every moment?

MORNING REFLECTION

EVENING REFLECTION

November 21st　How can I make this minute—right now—be enough?

MORNING REFLECTION

EVENING REFLECTION

November 22nd   What am I irrationally afraid of losing?

MORNING REFLECTION

EVENING REFLECTION

November 23rd   Why is my power to choose so resilient and adaptable?

MORNING REFLECTION

EVENING REFLECTION

November 24th   How can I see my loved ones as gifts not possessions?

MORNING REFLECTION

EVENING REFLECTION

November 25th   Is more money really going to make things better?

MORNING REFLECTION

EVENING REFLECTION

WEEK XLVIII
BALANCE THE BOOKS OF LIFE DAILY

We journal as a way of gathering up life's experiences, insights, frustrations, unexpected struggles and triumphs, and more. In all of this we are making a reckoning of our progress on life's way. Seneca, whose father-in-law was in charge of keeping the books on Rome's granary, liked the metaphor of balancing life's books each day. Rather than postpone, our impulse each day should be to bring things, as much as possible, to completion. Why? Because we never know what tomorrow might bring. Epictetus, too, would tell his students that the important thing was that they had begun: begun to practice, learn, get better. Give yourself credit this week for the journey you are on—and reflect on how far you have come (and how far there is left to go).

"Let us prepare our minds as if we'd come to the very end of life. Let us postpone nothing. Let us balance life's books each day. Life's greatest flaw is that it's always imperfect, and a certain portion of it is postponed. The one who puts the finishing touches on their life each day is never short of time."

—SENECA, *MORAL LETTERS*, 101.7b–8a

"Believe me, it's better to produce the balance-sheet of your own life than that of the grain market."

—SENECA, *ON THE BREVITY OF LIFE*, 18.3b

"I am your teacher and you are learning in my school. My aim is to bring you to completion, unhindered, free from compulsive behavior, unrestrained, without shame, free, flourishing, and happy, looking to God in things great and small—your aim is to learn and diligently practice all these things. Why then don't you complete the work, if you have the right aim and I have both the right aim and right preparation? What is missing? . . . The work is quite feasible, and is the only thing in our power. . . . Let go of the past. We must only begin. Believe me and you will see."

—EPICTETUS, *DISCOURSES*, 2.19.29–34

November 26th   What petty comparisons am I bothering myself with?

MORNING REFLECTION

EVENING REFLECTION

November 27th   What sources of unrest can I tune out?

MORNING REFLECTION

EVENING REFLECTION

November 28th   What's bothering me that I haven't spoken up about?

MORNING REFLECTION

EVENING REFLECTION

November 29th   How can I be less agitated—and complain about it less, too?

MORNING REFLECTION

EVENING REFLECTION

November 30th   Am I ready to accept the pull of the universe?

MORNING REFLECTION

EVENING REFLECTION

December 1st   If I lived today as if it were my last, what would I do?

MORNING REFLECTION

EVENING REFLECTION

December 2nd   How can I make my actions count?

MORNING REFLECTION

EVENING REFLECTION

WEEK XLIX
BE STINGY WITH TIME

One of the most common sayings we hear is "life is short." It is—but as Seneca remarked, it's also plenty long if you know how to use it. The first step to that? Not giving so much of it away to other people. Becoming miserly about our time is a powerful exercise, which can keep us from squandering this nonrenewable resource. What in your life consumes a lot of time for no good purpose? What amusements and desires consume our time without giving us any good return? As you review that list, make a commitment to doing something about it. Life is short, after all; you don't have too much to spare.

"Were all the geniuses of history to focus on this single theme, they could never fully express their bafflement at the darkness of the human mind. No person would give up even an inch of their estate, and the slightest dispute with a neighbor can mean hell to pay; yet we easily let others encroach on our lives—worse, we often pave the way for those who will take it over. No person hands out their money to passersby, but to how many do each of us hand out our lives! We're tight-fisted with property and money, yet think too little of wasting time, the one thing about which we should all be the toughest misers."

—SENECA, *ON THE BREVITY OF LIFE*, 3.1–2

"It's not at all that we have too short a time to live, but that we squander a great deal of it. Life is long enough, and it's given in sufficient measure to do many great things if we spend it well. But when it's poured down the drain of luxury and neglect, when it's employed to no good end, we're finally driven to see that it has passed by before we even recognized it passing. And so it is—we don't receive a short life, we make it so."

—SENECA, *ON THE BREVITY OF LIFE*, 1.3–4A

December 3rd   What practical problems am I solving with this philosophy?

MORNING REFLECTION

EVENING REFLECTION

December 4th   What do I truly own?

MORNING REFLECTION

EVENING REFLECTION

December 5th   What unpleasant thoughts can I face and use to my advantage?

MORNING REFLECTION

EVENING REFLECTION

December 6th   What can I do to *live* now, while I still can?

MORNING REFLECTION

EVENING REFLECTION

December 7th   Can I love the hand Fate deals me?

MORNING REFLECTION

EVENING REFLECTION

December 8th　Are there any feelings I need to face?

MORNING REFLECTION

EVENING REFLECTION

December 9th   Are you saying no enough?

MORNING REFLECTION

EVENING REFLECTION

WEEK L
KEEP THE RHYTHM

Marcus Aurelius must have known that as emperor he was part of a grand and great history. As a philosopher, he also knew that all people are part of a rhythm pulsing through both history and their own lives, and he liked to remind himself to not lose that beat. Return to your philosophy, he would tell himself when he drifted. Don't give in to the distractions. In fact, he tried constantly to return to it. That kind of awareness (*prosochē*, paying special attention) is something he learned from reading Epictetus, who told his students that while none of us can be perfect, we can catch ourselves when we begin to slide, when we drift from where we should be. Can you feel that rhythm this week? Can you point to examples of when you really felt locked into it?

"Walk the long gallery of the past, of empires and kingdoms succeeding each other without number. And you can also see the future, for surely it will be exactly the same, unable to deviate from the present rhythm. It's all one whether we've experienced forty years or an aeon. What more is there to see?"

—Marcus Aurelius, *Meditations*, 7.49

"When forced, as it seems, by circumstances into utter confusion, get a hold of yourself quickly. Don't be locked out of the rhythm any longer than necessary. You'll be able to keep the beat if you are constantly returning to it."

—Marcus Aurelius, *Meditations*, 6.11

"When you let your attention slide for a bit, don't think you will get back a grip on it whenever you wish—instead, bear in mind that because of today's mistake everything that follows will be necessarily worse. . . . Is it possible to be free from error? Not by any means, but it is possible to be a person always stretching to avoid error. For we must be content to at least escape a few mistakes by never letting our attention slide."

—Epictetus, *Discourses*, 4.12.1; 19

December 10th   What are you getting in return for the time you spend so freely?

MORNING REFLECTION

EVENING REFLECTION

December 11th   Are you living with dignity and courage?

MORNING REFLECTION

EVENING REFLECTION

December 12th   Will I keep the rhythm of life, no matter the interruptions?

MORNING REFLECTION

EVENING REFLECTION

December 13th   Can I be grateful for the time I've been given?

MORNING REFLECTION

EVENING REFLECTION

December 14th   What will my life be a testament to?

MORNING REFLECTION

EVENING REFLECTION

December 15th   Am I going to get a little bit better today?

MORNING REFLECTION

EVENING REFLECTION

December 16th   What am I doing to build my self-confidence?

MORNING REFLECTION

EVENING REFLECTION

WEEK LI
STAKE YOUR CLAIM

We like to collect the sayings of great writers or of leaders we admire—they often become mantras for us on the path of life, providing guidance and assurance. But as Seneca reminds us, truth hasn't been monopolized. We need to spend some time and effort each week formulating our own wisdom, staking our own claims based on our study, practice, and training. That's what this journal is about. Reflecting on the Stoic wisdom and adding our own to it. Seneca urged us to blaze our own trail and to take charge and stake our own claim. Well, let's do it. Let these pages reflect the insights you have learned by your own experiences. Let the inspiration you've taken from the Stoics create your own exercises, reminders, and perspectives.

> "For it's disgraceful for an old person, or one in sight of old age, to have only the knowledge carried in their notebooks. Zeno said this . . . what do you say? Cleanthes said that . . . what do you say? How long will you be compelled by the claims of another? Take charge and stake your own claim—something posterity will carry in its notebook."
>
> —SENECA, *MORAL LETTERS*, 33.7

> "Won't you be walking in your predecessors' footsteps? I surely will use the older path, but if I find a shorter and smoother way, I'll blaze a trail there. The ones who pioneered these paths aren't our masters, but our guides. Truth stands open to everyone, it hasn't been monopolized."
>
> —SENECA, *MORAL LETTERS*, 33.11

> "Don't act grudgingly, selfishly, without due diligence, or to be a contrarian. Don't overdress your thought in fine language. Don't be a person of too many words and too many deeds. . . . Be cheerful, not wanting outside help or the relief others might bring. A person needs to stand on their own, not be propped up."
>
> —MARCUS AURELIUS, *MEDITATIONS*, 3.5

December 17th   How well do I really know myself?

MORNING REFLECTION

EVENING REFLECTION

December 18th   The end for us all is clear, but is my purpose?

MORNING REFLECTION

EVENING REFLECTION

December 19th   What can I focus on that is much, much bigger than me?

MORNING REFLECTION

EVENING REFLECTION

December 20th   What am I really so afraid of?

MORNING REFLECTION

EVENING REFLECTION

December 21st   How can I make the most of today—and in doing so, my life?

MORNING REFLECTION

EVENING REFLECTION

December 22nd   What wisdom will I create today?

MORNING REFLECTION

EVENING REFLECTION

December 23rd   If I relaxed my tight grip on life, what would happen?

MORNING REFLECTION

EVENING REFLECTION

WEEK LII
TURN WORDS INTO WORKS

Marcus spent a great deal of time on his journals, yet within their pages we find him admonishing himself to throw them away, to never read their pages. Why? Because he didn't want them to be an excuse from the essential tasks at hand. The art of living will never be found anywhere but in our own efforts to be a good person. Never forget that is the aim of this journal. It is not to fill up pages with pretty thoughts but to inspire you to take action, to turn the words, as Seneca said, into works. In that we have the perfect place to end this year, with the ultimate Stoic prompt: Get active in your own rescue.

> "Stop wandering about! You aren't likely to read your own note-books, or ancient histories, or the anthologies you've collected to enjoy in your old age. Get busy with life's purpose, toss aside empty hopes, get active in your own rescue—if you care for yourself at all—and do it while you can."
>
> —MARCUS AURELIUS, *Meditations*, 3.14

> "You have proof in the extent of your wanderings that you never found the art of living anywhere—not in logic, nor in wealth, fame, or in any indulgence. Nowhere. Where is it then? In doing what human nature demands. How is a person to do this? By having principles be the source of desire and action. What principles? Those to do with good and evil, indeed in the belief that there is no good for a human being except what creates justice, self-control, courage, and freedom, and nothing evil except what destroys these things."
>
> —MARCUS AURELIUS, *Meditations*, 8.1.(5)

> "All study of philosophy and reading should be for the purpose of living a happy life . . . we should seek precepts to help us, noble and courageous words that can become facts . . . we should learn them in a way that words become works."
>
> —SENECA, *MORAL LETTERS*, 108.35

December 24th   Can I consume less to make more room for virtue?

MORNING REFLECTION

EVENING REFLECTION

December 25th   Where can I find reinvigoration and balance?

MORNING REFLECTION

EVENING REFLECTION

December 26th   Where am I wasting life?

MORNING REFLECTION

EVENING REFLECTION

December 27th   Is my soul stronger than my body?

MORNING REFLECTION

EVENING REFLECTION

December 28th   In a hundred years, who will remember or be remembered?

MORNING REFLECTION

EVENING REFLECTION

December 29th   What am I grateful for?

MORNING REFLECTION

EVENING REFLECTION

December 30th   How can I bring a calm mind to tough situations?

MORNING REFLECTION

EVENING REFLECTION

December 31st   How will I turn these words into works?

MORNING REFLECTION

EVENING REFLECTION

MORE STOIC PROMPTS

While this journal was designed to be the ultimate companion for *The Daily Stoic*, and *The Daily Stoic* was designed to be read as many times as a reader would like, you might well be looking for even more prompts and Stoic readings, especially if this is your second go around with the journal. That is something we are happy to provide.

First, we send out a free e-mail every single day of Stoic wisdom at DailyStoic.com. If you haven't signed up yet, you absolutely should!

Second, if you're looking for some classic and modern Stoic texts to journal along to, we have some recommendations:

- *Meditations* by Marcus Aurelius (we strongly recommend the Gregory Hays translation for Modern Library)
- *Letters of a Stoic* by Seneca (the abridged Penguin Classics edition is wonderful and there is also a full—and free—e-book edition put out by Tim Ferriss)
- *Discourses and Selected Writings* by Epictetus (again, hard to do better than Penguin Classics)
- *The Inner Citadel: The Meditations of Marcus Aurelius* by Pierre Hadot (this is a wonderful deep dive into Marcus Aurelius's philosophy and what makes him tick)
- *The Moral Sayings of Publilius Syrus: A Roman Slave* by Publilius Syrus (another slave turned philosopher whose pithy epigrams will give you something to write about each day)

If you want to learn more about Stoic exercises and practices, and their purpose, we like the following sources:

- Chapter 3 in Pierre Hadot's *Philosophy as a Way of Life: Spiritual Exercises from Socrates to Foucault* (Wiley-Blackwell, 1995)
- Chapters 15–16 in Richard Sorabji's *Emotion and Peace of Mind: From Stoic Agitation to Christian Temptation* (Oxford University Press, 2000)

- Part Two of Donald Robertson's *The Philosophy of Cognitive Behavioural Therapy: Stoic Philosophy as Rational and Cognitie Psychotherapy* (Karnac Books, 2010) or his equally excellent *Stoicism and the Art of Happiness* (Hodder & Stoughton, 2013)
- Part III of Massimo Pigliucci's *How to Be a Stoic: Using Ancient Philosophy to Live a Modern Life* (Basic Books, 2017)

For a broad selection of Stoic reading beyond the titles above, we have compiled the following list, which is continually being revised and added to at www.dailystoic.com/books-on-stoicism:

- James B. Stockdale's *Courage Under Fire: Testing Epictetus's Doctrines in the Laboratory of Human Behavior* (Hoover Institution Press, 1993)
- James Romm's *Dying Every Day: Seneca at the Court of Nero* (Vintage, 2014)
- Rob Goodman and Jimmy Soni's *Rome's Last Citizen: The Life and Legacy of Cato, Mortal Enemy of Caesar* (St. Martin's Griffin, 2014)
- Tom Wolfe's *A Man in Full* (Dial Press, 2001)
- William B. Irvine's *A Guide to the Good Life: The Ancient Art of Stoic Joy* (Oxford University Press, 2008)
- Alain de Botton's *The Consolations of Philosophy* (Vintage, 2001)
- Nassim Nicholas Taleb's *Antifragile: Things that Gain from Disorder* (Random House, 2014)
- James Miller's *Examined Lives: From Socrates to Nietzsche* (Picador, 2012)
- Nancy Sherman's *Stoic Warriors: The Ancient Philosophy Behind the Military Mind* (Oxford University Press, 2007)
- John Sellar's *Stoicism* (University of California Press, 2006)
- R. W. Sharples's *Stoics, Epicureans, and Skeptics: An Introduction to Hellenistic Philosophy* (Routledge, 1996)
- M. Andrew Holowchak's *The Stoics: A Guide for the Perplexed* (Bloomsbury Academic, 2008)
- F. H. Sandbach's *The Stoics* (Hackett Publishing Company, Inc., 1994)

- Margaret Graver's *Stoicism and Emotion* (University of Chicago Press, 2009)
- Brad Inwood's *The Cambridge Companion to the Stoics* (Cambridge University Press, 2003)
- Ronald Pies's *Everything Has Two Handles: The Stoic's Guide to the Art of Living* (Hamilton Books, 2008)
- Jules Evans's *Philosophy for Life and Other Dangerous Situations* (New World Library, 2013)
- Lawrence C. Becker's *A New Stoicism: Revised Edition* (Princeton University Press, 2017)
- Emily Wilson's *The Greatest Empire: A Life of Seneca* (Oxford University Press, 2014)

Interested in learning even more about stoicism?
Visit DailyStoic.com to sign up for a daily email,
engage in discussion, get advice, and more.

Join millions of other readers with these #1 bestsellers!

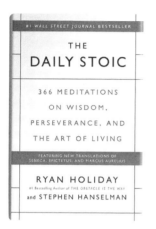

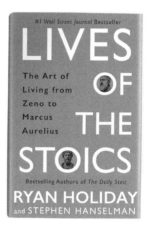

PORTFOLIO
PENGUIN

Penguin
Random
House

.

Portfolio/Penguin
An imprint of Penguin Random House LLC
375 Hudson Street
New York, New York 10014

Most Portfolio books are available at a discount when purchased in quantity for sales promotions or corporate use. Special editions, which include personalized covers, excerpts, and corporate imprints, can be created when purchased in large quantities. For more information, please call (212) 572-2232 or e-mail specialmarkets@penguinrandomhouse.com. Your local bookstore can also assist with discounted bulk purchases using the Penguin Random House corporate Business-to-Business program. For assistance in locating a participating retailer, e-mail B2B@penguinrandomhouse.com.

Library of Congress Cataloging-in-Publication Data

Names: Holiday, Ryan, author.
Title: The daily stoic journal : 366 days of writing and reflection on the art of living / Ryan Holiday.
Description: New York : Portfolio, 2017.
Identifiers: LCCN 2017060837 | ISBN 9780525534396 (hardcover)
Subjects: LCSH: Stoics. | Authorship. | Diaries—Authorship.
Classification: LCC B528 .H653 2017 | DDC 188—dc23
LC record available at https://lccn.loc.gov/2017060837

Printed in the United States of America
6th Printing

Book design by Daniel Lagin